POC

LET'S SIGN POCKET DICTIONARY
BSL Concise Beginner's Guide

Written and Illustrated
by

CATH SMITH

CO - SIGN
COMMUNICATIONS

CO-SIGN COMMUNICATIONS

First published 2005

ISBN 0 9542384 6 X

Published by Co-Sign Communications (DEAFSIGN)
16 Highfield Crescent, Hartburn,
Stockton-on-Tees TS18 5HH
Tel: 01642 580505 Fax: 01642 808959
email: cath@deafsign.com   www: deafsign.com

Distributed by Forest Books
The New Building, Ellwood Road, Milkwall,
Coleford, Gloucestershire   GL16 7LE
Tel: 01594 833858 Fax: 01594 833446
email: forest@forestbooks.com
www.ForestBooks.com

Printed in Great Britain by BAS
17 Southview, Bear Park Durham, DH7 7DE

ACKNOWLEDGEMENTS

(The signs contained in this book are taken from the ongoing work on our big Let's Sign Dictionary involving the people detailed below).

My grateful thanks and appreciation for;

Help and advice at various times and at various stages on different projects that have helped to develop the bank of graphics that now form this dictionary, particularly for their work on the Level 1 sign vocabulary and materials to;

The Middlesbrough British Sign Language Tutor Group;

Susan Eastwood, Marie Greenan, Pauline Hodgson, Roy Mitchell, Sandra Teasdale, Pat Topliss, Tracy Ward and Keith Williams, and to Barbara Casson of Middlesbrough Adult Education Service.

A special thank you to Sandra Teasdale for her help with the Early Years vocabulary,
to Keith Williams for checking the illustrations and to Pat Topliss for detailed checking of content and layout.

Cathy Murray and colleagues of Jobcentre Plus for their help with vocabulary for Let's Sign for Work.

Kath Keogan, Registered British Sign Language/English Interpreter for help in checking the vocabulary.

*Help with converting all original illustrations from bitmap to vector format for
Let's Sign & Write BSL Graphics for Sign Bilingual Materials to;*
Cate Detheridge of SymData, on behalf of Widgit Software.

Preparing the book for publication, innovating new working methods, and printing;
Stephen Smith, BAS, Durham.

Technical support;
Tony Huck and Tony Elsdon.

All the support at home;
My husband David and son William

CONTENTS

INTRODUCTION

The best way to learn British Sign Language (BSL) is through sign language classes taught by *Deaf tutors in face to face contact and it is strongly recommended that this book, as with our other publications, is used to support such learning.

This pocket book contains over 1,000 of the recently developed sign graphics from our large A4 format **LET'S SIGN Dictionary** in this handy reference book for easy use wherever you are.

The Introduction has been written for beginners new to signing, with illustrated examples and useful reference pages of numbers, days and months.

However, the signs it contains have been selected to provide a good core vocabulary for **all** users, in addition to specific signs for use with babies and early years, employment and inclusive school settings and BSL courses, making it a valuable text for learners at all stages.

The large **Let's Sign Dictionary** will continue to be the main comprehensive collection of signs for BSL learners and will be frequently added to and updated. Work with BSL tutors continues and your feedback and suggestions for inclusion are always welcome.

* The convention of the upper case 'D' in *Deaf* refers to people who identify themselves as culturally Deaf sign language users.

SOME QUESTIONS AND ANSWERS

Do all deaf people use sign language?

British Sign Language (BSL) is the indigenous natural language of the British Deaf community to whom it belongs. It has its own vocabulary with structures and grammar that are distinct from spoken language.

It is estimated that 60,000 people who are deaf from birth or early childhood form the nucleus of the Deaf sign language using community. BSL is essential to and greatly valued within the community and regarded by most members as their first natural language.

Added to this figure are large numbers of hearing people who may be Deaf family members, friends and colleagues and deaf people who use signs to support speech, who also use BSL on a regular basis.

The largest group of deaf people - the estimated 8,7000,000 people, who have lost all or part of their hearing after spoken language and a hearing identity have been established, are likely to use speech/lipreading/writing as their main means of communication.

Some deafened and hard of hearing people may decide to learn sign language but spoken language is their first language and likely to remain so.

Is sign language universal?

This is a popular idea and sign languages are certainly used world wide wherever groups of deaf people and children come together, but they are not all the same language.

Sign languages from different countries share the characteristics and spatial structures of visual gestural languages. This gives all natural sign languages a familiar look and feel to them and gives them more in common with each other than with spoken languages. However they each have their own rules and vocabularies and are distinct and separate languages.

Are other sign languages used in this country?

BSL is used in England, Scotland, Wales and Northern Ireland. The structures and grammar can be recognised throughout Britain. Most of the signs used are the same throughout but there are also strong regional differences similar to dialect and accent in spoken languages - numbers and colours are examples that have have many variations.

BSL also forms the basis of other systems such as Makaton and Signalong which have been developed to support language and communication with children and adults who have different special needs. Both systems use BSL sign vocabulary to support spoken language.

Is BSL taught in schools?

People often express surprise to discover that BSL has only been officially recognised by the government since 2003 and that its use in deaf education only re-emerged in the last 20 years. BSL was in use by deaf children in schools despite policies against it that were based on the belief that signing would stop deaf children developing speech.

From profoundly Deaf co-writer of Let's Sign Early Years, Sandra Teasdale (translated from BSL).......

.....BSL is my first language, even though my parents and family didn't sign and I had very little access to it when I was small. It is the language that feels natural and comfortable to me and the only way I can express myself properly. Like my Deaf friends and colleagues, English is not easy for me.

Not all of the children at the school were totally deaf, there was a real mixture just as there is today. Some had a lot of hearing and speech and used their hearing aids to communicate in this way - they were lost without them. Others had some useful hearing that they could use in some situations, but needed lip-reading (and signs) to help too - some could speak quite clearly and others couldn't. ....The important thing is that we all signed - and those who spoke still spoke - signing never stopped them.

Attitudes to BSL and teaching methods and policies have undergone great change in the past 15 or so years. The use of signing is now believed to benefit a whole range of children; pre-verbal hearing babies, children who are autistic, dyslexic, have specific speech/language difficulties or learning disability, in addition to sign language proper for deaf children.

The visual and kinaesthetic elements involved in signing certainly add new dimensions and alternative channels to help children internalise and take pleasure in language use, and whole group or class involvement is a way of ensuring a rich and inclusive communication environment.

Most children are like linguistic sponges, with innate ability for communication and language acquisition. Not only that, but children do seem to love to sign. There can be little doubt that as a general life skill, it offers all children the potential of improved language and communication skills and to have some confidence and awareness to meet the communication needs of others - it's always going to be an extra string to their bow.

A hope for the future is to see BSL as part of the school curriculum with lead bodies from the Deaf community developing the curriculum, providing the materials and delivering the teaching. Let's sign!

THE DRAWINGS: The Face

The drawings show the important components of the signs as clearly as possible without distracting background details. One of the most important of these components is the face.

Learners typically focus on the hands and their movements in the early stages, and tend to neglect the importance of the face. Communication in BSL however starts with eye contact, and the face is the focal point throughout.

Signing can be dull or even meaningless without good and appropriate facial clues or if part of the face is obscured by dark glasses, beard, or moustache for example.

The facial expressions and upper body postures in the drawings are appropriate to some signs in some contexts, but not all the possibilities can be shown. BSL uses a range of eye, mouth, face and body movements that have grammatical functions in that they can add to, modify or change meaning.

These are termed *non-manual features*, as in the sign on the next page and they are referred to and described in the captions where space permits.

Some excellent photographic examples and details of BSL grammar can be found in the British Deaf Association's *Dictionary of British Sign Language/English* and in Sutton-Spence and Woll's *The Linguistics of British Sign Language*, both of which are detailed in Sources and Recommended Reading on page 378.

NON-MANUAL FEATURES: The Face

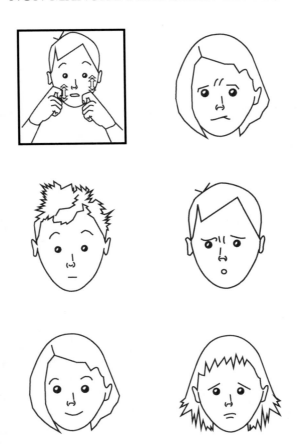

BASIC HANDSHAPES

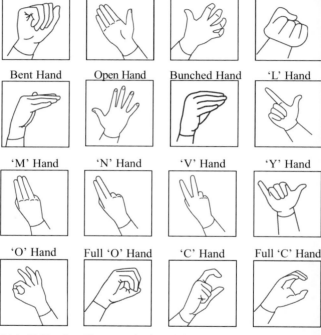

Closed Hand   Flat Hand   Clawed Hand   Fist

Bent Hand   Open Hand   Bunched Hand   'L' Hand

'M' Hand   'N' Hand   'V' Hand   'Y' Hand

'O' Hand   Full 'O' Hand   'C' Hand   Full 'C' Hand

Irish 'T Hand

Frequently used handshapes in BSL and terms used in this book to describe them.

The fingers are identified (from the thumb) as *index, middle finger, ring finger* and *little finger.*

GUIDE TO HEADINGS AND CAPTIONS

Orientation, direction and movement

The direction the hands may face, point or move are described as if the hands are open.

As illustrated below the R. hand is palm left and the L. hand is palm right. They can also be described as palm facing, or palm in.

The hands may be described as *'pointing'* up, forward etc even if the fingers are bent in a different direction or closed.

As illustrated, both hands are pointing forward, palms facing.

If the handshapes are described for example as *index, and thumb extended*, then it is understood that the other fingers are closed.

Diagonal movements are described *'forward/left'* or *'back/right'* and so on.

HEADINGS AND CAPTIONS

Languages have very few direct word for word or sign for word equivalents between each other, and the headings given for each sign are a guide to meaning rather than a direct translation.

Some words have many possible ways of being signed and some signs have many different word/phrase equivalent meanings.

Where possible, more than one word heading is given, to give a clearer idea of a sign's meaning and context.

The captions are intended to give extra information on the handshape, location and movement of signs as described on the previous page.

The captions also give details of non-manual features (face and body language). Changes in context are given when relevant and where space allows. Details of changes in *direction* and of different *variations*, are given in *bold italics*. Additional meanings are given in **BOLD CAPITALS**.

All signs are described and illustrated as if the signer is right-handed, with the right hand always referred to as R. and the left hand as L. Left-handed signers will use the reverse of this, with the left hand as dominant. From the thumb, the fingers are referred to as index, middle, ring and little finger.

SAME WORD - DIFFERENT MEANING - DIFFERENT SIGN

LIKE

eg I *like* that.

In the dictionary, this sign is headed **LIKE, FOND OF.**

LIKE

eg just *like* you.

This sign is headed **LIKE, SAME AS.**

Headings clarify and give additional meanings of each sign.

LIGHT

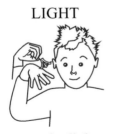

eg put the *light* on.

Headed **LIGHT, PUT LIGHT ON.**

LIGHT

eg it's still *light*.

Headed **LIGHT, DAY, DAWN.**

Some examples have the same general meaning but the specifics in context are different, requiring the sign to change. In **FOLLOW** for example, the upright index fingers represent people and the flat hands represent vehicles. This information is given in the caption as well as clued by the heading for each entry.

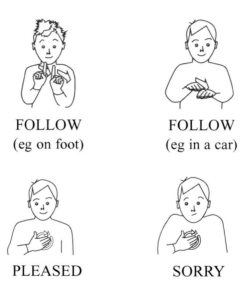

FOLLOW
(eg on foot)

FOLLOW
(eg in a car)

PLEASED

SORRY

The last 2 signs illustrate what might at first appear to be the same sign. The appropriate non-manual features of the face and body clearly differentiate the meanings and demonstrate their central role in BSL.

FINGERSPELLING IN BSL

Many people think that sign language consists just of
fingerspelling. It is an important and integrated part
of BSL, but its use varies considerably between
individuals. Appropriate use needs to be learned just
as any part of the language.

- It represents letters of the English alphabet.
- It provides a direct link to English.
- It relies on knowledge of English.
- It is commonly used to spell out names of
  people and places.
- Fluently spelt words are read as patterns.
- Some signers use it to spell out small commonly
  used words eg SON, DAY, IF (even though these
  words have signs).
- Repeated initials are common eg 'KK'
  kitchen, 'FF' father, 'TT' toilet.
- Abbreviations and contractions are also common
  eg 'BHM' Birmingham, 'BL' Bristol, as are
  acronyms eg BBC, NHS.

The drawings give a static image of the letters, but
they may blend and look quite different when in
fluent use and need a lot of practice to read back full
word patterns.

BRITISH
FINGERSPELLING
ALPHABET
LEFT-HANDED VERSION

BRITISH
FINGERSPELLING
ALPHABET
RIGHT-HANDED VERSION

FINGERSPELLING: Days of the Week

Days of the week are commonly based on fingerspelling. These are usually abbreviated forms as shown in the illustrations opposite.

In addition to the example of MONDAY represented by 'MON', a repeated 'MM' is also alternatively used.

TUESDAY may be represented by 'TU' 'TT', or 'TUES', WEDNESDAY by 'WED' or 'WW', THURSDAY by 'TH', and FRIDAY by 'FRI' or 'FF', and other similar variations.

SUNDAY can be signed as in the last illustration with the flat hands tapping together twice, although SATURDAY and SUNDAY do have alternative signs in some regions.

Months of the year are similarly fingerspelt abbreviations or the shorter words are spelt in full, eg MAY, JUNE.

A separate 'days of the week' system is mainly used in Scotland. The index finger and thumb close together twice for MONDAY, the middle finger and thumb for TUESDAY, the ring finger and thumb for WEDNESDAY and little finger and thumb for THURSDAY.

FRIDAY is signed with R. palm left 'V' hand moving right to left across the chin. SATURDAY is a repeated downward opening movement of a closed hand held under the chin, and SUNDAY is palm left R. flat hand bending back to contact upper chest twice. SATURDAY and SUNDAY also have alternative versions in some regions.

DAYS OF THE WEEK

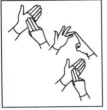

MONDAY

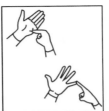

TUESDAY

WEDNESDAY

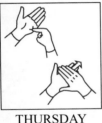

THURSDAY

FRIDAY

SATURDAY

There are other variations for signing days of the week, but these are commonly used and understood examples used in BSL.

SUNDAY

FINGERSPELLING: Months of the Year

Months are usually fingerspelt either in full or contracted forms as in the examples below. The months follow left to right going down the pages.

 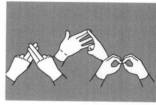

FINGERSPELLING: Months of the Year

There are other variations and patterns based on the fingerspelt word, but these examples are commonly used and understood.

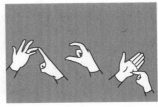

SIGNS INCORPORATING FINGERSPELLING

Some signs are based on initial letters or incorporate letters into the sign.

Daughter

Dictionary
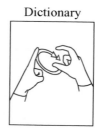

Father

Mother/Mum

Mother/Mum

Kitchen
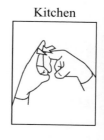

Toilet

Year

Natural
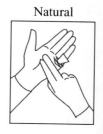

SIGNS INCORPORATING FINGERSPELLING

Initial letter may be repeated or located/ moved in sign-like ways.

Confidence

Qualification

Community

Million

Video

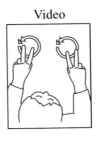

TV

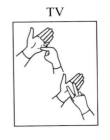

Gold

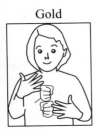

Manchester

Newcastle

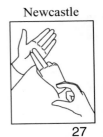

NUMBERS: Quick Reference Guide

Numbers are notorious for their regional variations.
It is not possible to show them all in this simple guide,
but the two most commonly used and understood
systems are illustrated. Learners need to be aware of
their own and other regional signs.

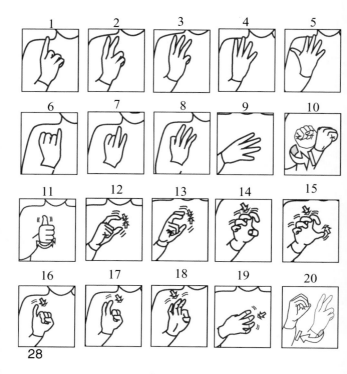

20 is illustrated - 30, 40, 50, 60 etc start with the relevant number handshape for 3, 4, 5, (6 and so on from either system) followed by zero, up to 90.

Other numbers over 20, sign the first digit then the second ie 2 then 1 as in 21 shown on the right and so on with the relevant numbers from your regional system.

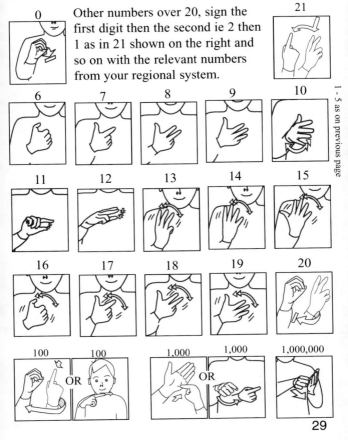

ABLE, ABILITY, CAN

Palm back 'C' hand in front of face moves forward/down, as index flexes or closes onto thumb.

ABOUT, APPROXIMATELY

Palm down open hand moves round in circular movement.

ABOUT, CONCERNING

Edge of R. closed hand with extended index rubs in small circles on L. palm. *Varies*.

ABOVE, HIGHER THAN

R. bent hand moves upwards in small arc to finish above L. Also means **SUPERIOR.**

ABROAD, FOREIGN

R. bent hand makes two short forward movements against L. hand.

ABSENT, OFF, AWAY

Flat hand is held palm back in front of body, and swings forward twisting to palm down.

ABUSE, VIOLATE

R. fist brushes side to side several times against L. index finger.   The lips are stretched

ACCEPT, RECEIVE, GET

Palm up hands (or one hand) move back to body with closing grasping movement.

ACCESS, GO THROUGH

Fingers of R. flat hand move forward/left between fingers of L. hand.

ACCIDENT

Fingerspell 'ACC' with R. hand moving to the right in small hops. *Varies*.

ACCIDENT, OOPS, SORRY

Clawed hand makes small shaking movements near side of head or chin. *Varies*. Also means MISTAKE.

ACCOUNTS, ACCOUNTANT

Fingers wiggle as palm back hands move alternately up and down. Also means FIGURES.

ACCURATE, EXACT

'O' hand makes short firm movement forward/down, lips pressed together. Also means **METICULOUS**.

ACCUSE, BLAME

Fingers point and jab sharply towards the person referred to (*directional*) eyes narrowed.

ACHIEVE, SUCCEED

Palm back closed hands with thumbs up twist sharply from wrists to palm down. *Varies.*

ACHIEVE/MENT, SUCCESS

Irish 'T' hand twists in small circular movements at head height. Also means **VICTORY, WIN**. *Varies.*

ACT, DRAMA, ROLE PLAY

Palm forward 'O' hands move alternately backwards and forwards on chest several times. Also means **PERFORM/ANCE**.

ADD, ADD UP, COUNT

Palm back hands move upwards and forwards with fingers wiggling.

ADD, EXTRA, PLUS

R. bent hand moves over in tipping movement into L. palm. Also means **SUPPLEMENT**.

ADDRESS, LIVE

Tip of middle finger (or clawed hand) rubs up and down on side of chest.

ADOPT, TAKE, TAKEAWAY

Palm down open hand moves in towards the body as the fingers close in grasping action.

ADULT, GROWN-UP

Bent hand moves firmly upwards near head height. Cheeks may be puffed. Also means **GIANT**.

ADVANTAGE, GAIN

Tips of 'O' hand twist over and brush down side of upper chest.

ADVERT, PRINT

R. closed hand twists over to contact L. palm and back again.

ADVICE, ADVISE/R

R. index moves from mouth then becomes closed hand with thumb up on L. palm and hands move forward in small arc.

AEROPLANE, FLY, FLIGHT

Closed hand with thumb and little finger extended moves in action of a plane flying.

AFRAID, TERRIFIED

Clawed hands tap on chest twice, as body makes slight backward, cowering movement.

AFTER, AFTERWARDS

Palm down R. closed hand with thumb out moves over L. in small arc. Flat hand can be used. Also means **THEN**. *Varies*.

AFTER, LATER

Palm forward index finger moves sideways in small arc. Movement may repeat. *Varies*.

AFTERNOON

Tips of 'N' hand touch chin, then hand twists from wrist to point forwards.

AGAIN, REPEAT, OFTEN

Palm left 'V' hand makes short quick shaking movements forward/down from the wrist. Also means **FREQUENTLY.**

AGE, AGED

Fingers of palm back hand wiggle in front of nose. Also means **HOW OLD?** (with raised or furrowed eyebrows).

AGENDA, LIST, ORDER

Extended thumb moves down from L. palm in small wiggling movements. *Varies.*

AGREE, AGREEMENT

Closed hands with thumbs up contact knuckles together. The head nods. Also means **APPROPRIATE**.

AIM, DIRECT, TARGET

R. flat hand moves forward towards extended L. index finger held forward.

ALARM, BELL (clock, fire)

Extended R. index finger bangs several times against the L. palm. Index waggles forward/down for **CLOCK**.

ALIVE, LIFE

Tip of middle finger (or clawed hand) rubs up and down on side of chest. Also a *regional* sign for **TOILET**.

ALL, EVERY, EVERYBODY

Flat hand sweeps sideways.

ALL GONE, NO MORE

Palm up hands move apart in small arc as shoulders shrug. (Child appropriate sign). *Varies*.

ALL RIGHT, OK, FINE

Closed hand with thumb up and pointing out moves in small outward circles. Both hands can be used.

ALLOW, LET, PERMIT

Index fingers point towards each other, then shake down/apart twice, or palm up flat hands move forward.

ALONE, SINGLE, UNIQUE

Palm back R. index finger moves down and to the right behind L. palm.

ALREADY, PREPARED

Thumb tips of open hands (or just one hand) make small upward brushing movements on upper chest.

ALSO, TOO, AS WELL

Index fingers pointing forward touch together twice.

ALWAYS, REGULAR

Extended R. thumb moves to the left behind L. flat hand. Also means USUAL.

AMERICA/N, USA

Hands with fingers intermeshed move round in horizontal circle.

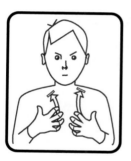

ANGRY, CROSS, FURIOUS

Clawed hands (or just one hand) move up body sharply to palm up, cheeks puffed, brows furrowed. Also means **MAD, TEMPER**.

ANIMAL

Clawed hands make repeated forward circular movements. Also means **CRAWL/ER**.

ANOTHER, ELSE, OTHER

R. index finger makes repeated upward brushing movements against back of L. middle fingertip.

ANSWER, REPLY

Tip of extended R. index finger brushes backwards in repeated circular movements off tip of L. thumb.

ANXIOUS, UNEASY

Clawed hand makes repeated circles on the lower abdomen.

ANY, ANYONE, ANYTHING

Closed hand (or both hands) with thumb and little finger extended moves sideways with repeated waggling movement.

ANYWAY, NEVER MIND

Hands brush alternately backwards and forwards against each other. Also means **NEVERTHELESS**.

APOLOGISE, APOLOGY

Fingertips of R. hand contact lips, then rub in circular movements on L. palm.

APPEAL, SUE

Irish 'T' hand moves forward/down twisting from the wrist (*directional*). Also means **SUSPEND, PROSECUTE**.

APPLE

Full 'C' hand twists upwards and forwards from the wrist near the mouth like taking a bite.

APPOINT, EMPLOY

Full 'C' hand moves inwards from the side. Also means **SUBSTITUTE, SUPPLY**.

APPOINT, EMPLOY

Index fingers pointing forward move forward/left together. *Varies.*

APPROVE, CONFIRM

Closed hands with thumbs up twist over and inwards to palm down. Also means **BLESS, RATIFY.**

ARGUE, QUARREL, ROW

Index and middle fingers extended and bent; hands face each other and move up and down alternately.

ARITHMETIC, MATHS

Palm back hands move up and down alternately as fingers wiggle. Also means CALCULATE, SUMS.

ARMY, MILITARY, FORCES

Edge of R. flat hand contacts left, then right upper chest.

ARRANGE, SORT OUT

Hands twist from wrists alternately backwards and forwards brushing against each other.

ARRIVE, REACH, GET TO

R. bent hand moves in forward arc to contact L. palm held forward.

ART, DRAW

Palm back 'N' hand moves down in front of face in side to side wiggling movement.

ASIAN, ETHNIC

Fingers of palm back R. hand rub in circular movements on back of L.

ASK, REQUEST, ENQUIRE

'O' hand moves forward from mouth or in *direction* to suit context.

ASSESS, ASSESSOR

Palm down 'N' hands (or flat hands) move up and down alternately. Can also be palm up.

ASYLUM SEEKER

Bent R. hand makes two short forward movements over L. hand, then R. index finger makes sharp movement under L.

ATTEMPT, EFFORT, TRY

R. index brushes forward sharply against L.

ATTITUDE

Flat hand palm back in front of face twists to palm forward.

AUDIENCE

Clawed hands move back to body, or may be twisted round to face backwards and move forward. Also means **CONGREGATION**.

AUNTIE, AUNT

Tips of bent 'V' hand tap chin twice. Also one version of **UNCLE.**

AUTUMN

'N' hands move downwards with twisting movements from the wrists, like leaves falling.

AWAKE, WAKE UP

Index fingers flick open at sides of eyes. Also means **AWARE, AWARENESS.**

AWFUL, SERIOUS

Little fingers extended, make short forward repeated movements. Also means **SEVERE, UNFORTUNATE**.

BABY, DOLL

Arms move from side to side in rocking movements.

BACK OFF, BUTT OUT

Palm down bent hands pull back towards body. Also means **WITHDRAW**.

BACK UP, ADVOCACY

Closed hands with thumbs up, move forward together, one behind other. Also means **SUPPORT**.

BACON, RASHER

Index finger and thumb move apart and close together in outline shape of rasher of bacon.

BAD, WRONG, NAUGHTY

Extended little finger makes short movement forward. May repeat.

BAG, CARRIER, CASE

Palm back closed hand makes short repeated downward movements. May vary in context.

BAKE, BAKING, BAKER

Closed hands twist over several times simultaneously in action of kneading.

BAKED BEANS

Hands form repeated fingerspelt 'BB'.

BALL, FOOTBALL

Hands with fingers curved move round and apart in shape of large ball.

BAN, NOT ALLOWED

Fists start crossed, then pull sharply apart. Little fingers may be extended. Also means FORBID, TABOO.

BANANA

R. 'O' hand moves in peeling action of banana held in L. hand, or index fingers and thumbs move in outline shape.

BANK

R. closed hand bangs down onto L. palm

BASIC, ESTABLISH, SET UP

R. fist rests on back of L. hand as both hands make short firm movement down.

BATH, BATHE

Open hands move up and down chest several times. Closed hands can be used.

BATH, TOWEL

Closed hands move in action of holding and drying with a bath towel.

BEAUTIFUL, MARVELLOUS

Tips of bunched hand spring forward and open from the lips.

BECAUSE

R. flat hand contacts index edge of L. hand, then twists and moves left to touch inside of L. thumb.

BECAUSE, REASON

Edge of extended R. index finger taps side of left upper chest twice.

BED, SLEEP

Head tilts slightly to rest on flat hand. Can be both hands held palms together.

BEEN, FINISHED

Palm up flat hand twists with small downward flick to palm down.

BEFORE, EARLIER

R. closed hand with thumb extended moves in small backward arc over L. hand. *Varies.*

BEFORE, EARLIER, EARLY

R. flat hand moves from wrist up left forearm in small arc. *Varies.*

BEFORE, PAST, PREVIOUS

R. flat hand moves backwards over right shoulder several times.

BEGIN, START

Open hands palm down/back snap closed as hands twist to palm forward. *Varies.*

BEGIN, START

R. closed hand with thumb up moves sharply down behind L. flat hand. *Varies.*

BEHAVE, MANNER/S

Flat hands brush alternately down the body in backward downward circular movements.

BELIEVE, BELIEVER

Index finger contacts side of forehead then changes to flat hand edge down onto L. palm.

BELONG TO, CULTURE

Closed hand lands on L. palm and twists to palm forward or in direction of referent.

BENEFIT, DOLE, PENSION

Palm up clawed hand moves in towards body grasping closed to a fist in repeated movement.

BEST

Tip of R. extended thumb brushes forward sharply against top of L. extended thumb.

BETTER

Tip of R. extended thumb makes two small forward brushing movements against top of L. thumb.

BICYCLE, CYCLE, PEDAL

Closed hands (index fingers may be extended and bent) make alternate forward circular motions.

BIG, HUGE, MASSIVE

Open hands move apart in small arcs with emphasis. Cheeks may be puffed. Will *vary* in context of item referred to.

BIRD

Index finger and thumb open and close in front of mouth. Elbows may move in and out (**CHICKEN**).

BIRMINGHAM

Fingers open and close onto thumb as hand moves forward/right near mouth, or fingerspell **BHM**. *Varies.*

BIRTHDAY

Flat hands near sides of waist move forward/in and then upwards and apart. *Varies.*

BISCUIT

Tips of R. clawed hand tap twice against left elbow. May *vary.*

BLACK

Closed hand brushes forward/down on side of cheek. **Colours can vary widely.**

BLACKCURRANT

Closed hand brushes forward/down on side of cheek, then hand moves forward in 'C' shape. May *vary*.

BLANKET, BEDCLOTHES

Closed hands move slightly forwards, upwards and back onto body.

BLIND, BLINDNESS

Palm back 'V' hand (fingers may be bent) makes small side to side movements in front of eyes.

BLOOD, BLEED/ING

R. open hand brushes forward on top of L. Movement may repeat.

BLUE

Fingers of R. hand rub in small circles on L. palm or wrist. **Colours can vary widely.**

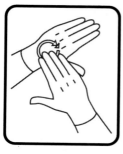

BLUE

R. hand rubs in small circles on back of L. **Colours can vary widely.** Also means **ASIAN** (L. hand may be palm back).

BOAT, FERRY, SAIL

Tips of flat hands touch, hands held at an angle move forwards in up and down bobbing movement.

BOIL, BOILING, BUBBLING

Palm back hands with index fingers up make small alternate upward circular movements like bubbles rising.

BOMB, EXPLOSION

Closed hands start crossed at wrists, then pull sharply apart twitsting to palms forward. Cheeks may be puffed.

BOOK, PASSPORT

Flat hands start palm to palm, then twist open and apart.

BOOK (to), APPOINTMENT

Closed hands come together to contact at the knuckles.

BOOK (to), CONTRACT

Tips of bent R. 'V' hand contact L. palm. *Varies.* Also means **RESERVE**.

BOOTS

Fists make upward pulling movements on right then left side near waist.

BORE/D, BORING, YAWN

Flat hand taps chin several times with mouth slightly open as if stifling a yawn.

BORN, BIRTH, DELIVER/Y

Palm up flat hands near sides of waist move forwards and towards each other.

BORROW, HIRE, LOAN

Closed hands held palm to palm and at an angle; hands move back to body in small arc.
Directional.

BOSS/Y, MANAGER, HEAD

Index fingers pointing forward/up twist sharply up/back from wrist.   May be one hand only.

BOTH, PAIR, COUPLE

Palm back 'V' hand shakes side to side several times.
Directional.

BOTTLE, DRINK (baby's)

Closed hand with thumb out tips upwards near the mouth.

BOX, PARCEL, PACKAGE

Flat hands held palm facing change to both palm back, one in front of other in box shape. Also *regional* sign for ROOM.

BOY, BOYFRIEND

Extended R. index finger brushes across chin to the left. May repeat. *Varies.* Also means RUSSIA/N.

BOY, BOYFRIEND

Index finger and thumb stroke down chin closing together twice. *Varies.*

BRAG, BOAST, SHOW OFF

Shoulders waggle as thumbs brush alternately down chest in backward circular movements.

BRAVE, BRAVERY

Tips of clawed hand touch chin, then hand makes short firm movement forward. *Varies.*

BREAD, LOAF

Edge of R. flat hand moves in slicing action across L. palm. *Varies.*

BREAK, FRACTURE, SNAP

Fists held together twist apart in snapping action.

BREAK, LEISURE, REST

Thumb tips of open hands (or one hand) on chest, fingers may wiggle. Head may tilt. Also means **RELAX.**

BREAKFAST, LUNCH, TEA

Bunched hand makes two short movements to the mouth. Also means **SUPPER.**

BRIEF, ABBREVIATE

Closed hands with thumbs out make short abrupt movement towards each other.

BRING, FETCH

Irish 'T' hands move simultaneously from right to left in small arc, or in *direction* to suit context.

BRITAIN, BRITISH

Palm down open hands make short repeated downward movements. Also means **SETTLE DOWN.**

BROTHER

Knuckles of closed hands rub up and down against each other. Thumbs may be extended. Also one version of **MILK.**

BROWN

R. hand rubs in small circles on left forearm. **Colours can vary widely.**

BRUSH (hair)

Closed hand moves in action of brushing hair near side of head. Different types of brush are signed differently.

BRUSH UP, POLISH

Knuckles of R. closed hand rub backwards and forwards along extended L. index finger.

BUILD/ING, CONSTRUCT

Hands move up brushing against the hand above alternately several times.

BULLY, ABUSE, PROVOKE

Extended index fingers make circular alternate jabbing movements in *direction* to suit context.

BURGER, HAMBURGER

Clawed hands make two short movements towards each other.

BUS, LORRY, TRUCK, VAN

Palm up closed hands make wide flat steering movements. Also means **DRIVER.**

BUS, TUBE

Fingers of bent 'V' hand make short movement forward at shoulder height (*regional*).

BUSY, HARD WORK

R. flat hand swivels forward/down over back of L. Cheeks may be puffed.

BUTTER, SPREAD

Edge of R. 'N' hand makes several small repeated scraping movements along L. palm.

BUTTERFLY, MOTH

Hands are crossed with thumbs interlocked, and hands bend from wrists in flapping movements.

BUY, PURCHASE

R. Irish 'T' hand brushes downwards across L. palm. *Varies.*

BYE, GOODBYE, CHEERIO

Hand moves side to side in waving movement, or flat hand bends repeatedly from palm knuckle.

CAKE, BUN, SCONE

Tips of R. clawed hand tap twice on back of L. hand. Also means **ROLL**, **SMALL PIE**.

CAN, COULD, POSSIBLE

Index finger and thumb close together in front of nose. May open and close several times. Also means **POTENTIAL**.

CAN'T, COULDN'T, UNABLE

Index finger moves down and loops over like crossing something out as head shakes. Also **IMPOSSIBLE** (two hands).

CANCEL, BAN

Tip of R. index finger draws a cross on L. palm. Also means **VOTE, BALLOT**.

CAR, DRIVE, DRIVER

Closed hands move in action of holding and moving a steering wheel.

CAR PARK

Edge of R. flat hand (vehicle classifier) contacts L. palm several times with small movements to the right, like cars in a row.

CARDIFF

Full 'C' hand contacts L. palm twice.

CARE FOR, LOOK AFTER

'V' hands one on top of the other move forward/down together from near eyes. Also means **CARETAKER**.

CAREFUL, TAKE CARE

'C' hands move forward/down from near eyes. Index fingers may start straight and flex as they move.

CARROT

Fist held at side of mouth makes sharp twisting movement as if holding and taking a bite from a carrot.

CAT, WHISKERS

Fingers flex as hands make short repeated outward movements from sides of mouth. *Varies.*

CATERPILLAR

Index finger moves forward flexing repeatedly.

CATHOLIC, CHRISTIAN

Tip of thumb draws a cross on the forehead. Also one version of **BAPTISE, CHRISTEN.**

CD-ROM

Knuckles of R. 'Y' hand contact L. palm as R. hand twists repeatedly from the wrist.

CELEBRATE, RAVE UP

'Y' hands twist repeatedly from wrists as arms move in circular waving movements. Cheeks may be puffed.

CENTRE, MIDDLE

Tip of R. middle finger taps twice into centre of L. palm.

CEREAL, BREAKFAST

Irish 'T' hand makes spooning actions up to the mouth. Also means **SPOON**, **PUDDING** and one version of **SOUP**.

CERTIFICATE, QUALIFY

'O' hands held apart, one higher than the other, make small repeated shaking movements.

CHAIR, SEAT, SIT DOWN

Palm down fists make short firm movement down. Elbows may be out.

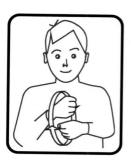

CHANGE, ADAPT, BECOME

Closed hands circle backwards round each other. *Varies.*

CHANGE, ALTER, CONVERT

Irish 'T' hands held palms facing twist round each other to finish crossed over. Can be signed with index fingers extended or closed hands. *Varies.*

CHARGE, COMMAND

R. hand bends sharply down from wrist while moving down and to the left. The movement may be across L. palm

CHEAP, INEXPENSIVE

Palm down R. 'N' hand moves sharply down towards palm up L.. 'N' hand.

CHECK, TEST, TRY OUT

Index moves down from eye, then 'Y' hands (or just one hand) move down in waggling movements from wrists.

CHEEK, CHEEKY

Bent index and thumb grasp cheek and make small shaking movements. Also **BARE, MEAT** (*regional*).

CHEESE

Fingertips of R. bent hand rest on L. palm as R. hand twists repeatedly from the wrist.

CHEMIST, PHARMACY

Extended R. little finger makes small circular movements in L. full 'C' hand. Also means **POISON**.

CHEQUE, NOTE, TICKET

Thumbs and index fingers move apart in outline shape, size may vary.

CHILD, TODDLER

Palm down flat hand makes short movement down. Also means **LOW, SOUTH**.

CHILDREN, TODDLERS

Palm down flat hand moves down, then repeats slightly to the side. Both hands can be used, moving apart.

CHIPS

Index and thumbs close together repeatedly in small outward movements indicating the outline shape.

CHOCOLATE

Edge of bent index finger brushes down chin twice. *Varies.*

CHOOSE, PICK, SELECT

Index finger closes onto thumb as hand moves backwards. May repeat, and with two hands alternately. *Directional.* Also means **INVITE**.

CHRISTMAS

R. hand brushes down across back of L. then closes and contacts back of L. hand again.

CHRISTMAS, SANTA

Fingers close onto thumb as they brush down chin and move down.

CHURCH, CHAPEL

Two fists, one on top of the other, move up and down several times.

CINEMA, FILM, MOVIE

R. open hand flickers repeatedly from side to side against L. index finger.

CLAIM

Flat hand moves sharply down/forward to finish palm up.

CLASH, FALL OUT, FIGHT

Closed hands, little fingers extended, move firmly together twisting to palm back. Also means **COINCIDE, CONFLICT**.

CLASS, CATEGORY

Full 'C' hands move in twisting at the wrists to touch together at fingertips.

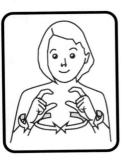

CLASS, CLASSROOM

'C' hands face each other then twist apart and round to finish touching with palms facing back.
Varies.

CLEAN, CLARIFY

Edge of R. flat hand brushes forward twice along L. palm.

CLEAN, CLEAR

R. hand moves forward/right along L. palm.

CLEAN/ING, HOUSEWORK

Closed hands make repeated alternate circular rubbing movements. Also means CLEANER, CHAR.

CLEVER, INTELLIGENT

Tip of extended thumb moves sharply left to right across the forehead. Cheeks may be puffed.

CLOCK

Extended R. index finger waggles forward/down against the L. palm .

CLOSE, SHUT

Flat hands swing backwards in closing action to touch at tips, finishing palm back. *Varies.*

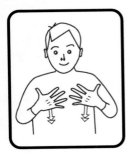

CLOTHES, CLOTHING

Open hands brush repeatedly down the body. Also means **DRESS, GET DRESSED.**

CLOUD, CLOUDY

Palm forward clawed hands make repeated alternate circling movements.

CO-ORDINATE, UNITE

Interlocked fingers of 'O' hands move round in circular movement. Also means **ASSOCIATE, CO-OPERATE**.

COACH, BUS

Full 'C' hands, one in front of the other, pull diagonally apart, forward/back.

COAT, JACKET

Closed hands move down
and round from shoulders
in action of putting coat on.

COCHLEAR IMPLANT

Tips of bent 'V' hand
contact side of head
above/behind the ear.

COFFEE

'C' hand makes short
quick twisting movements
near side of mouth or R.
fist grinds on top of L.
Varies.

COLD, FLU, HANKY

Fingers close onto thumb in wiping action near the nose.

COLD, FREEZING, WINTER

Closed hands and elbows pull into body in shivering action, shoulders hunched, cheeks puffed.

COLLEGE

'C' hand makes short quick twisting movements from the wrist near the side of forehead. *Varies.*

COLOUR

'C' hand makes anticlockwise circular movements. ***Varies.***

COLOUR

Palm forward open hand makes anticlockwise circular movements. ***Varies.***

COMB, COMB YOUR HAIR

Irish 'T' hand moves in action of using a hair comb.

COME, COME BACK

Index finger held forward moves back to body. Index finger may be bent or flex (**COME HERE**).

COMMUNICATE

Full 'C' hands (or 'C' hands) move backwards and forwards alternately. Also means **COMMUNICATION.**

COMMUNITY

R. 'C' hand sweeps round L. index finger from behind.

COMMUNITY CENTRE

Sign for **COMMUNITY** then sign for **CENTRE**; middle finger tip taps twice in centre of L. palm.

COMPANY, FACTORY, FIRM

Closed hands with thumbs up start together one behind the other, and move apart diagonally.

COMPETITION, FIXTURES

Index fingers make short movement towards each other several times as hands move down.

COMPLAIN, GRUMBLE

Fingertips of clawed hand brush upwards twice on chest. Brows are furrowed.

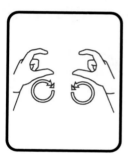

COMPUTER

'C' hands move in small simultaneous circular movements. May be combined with next sign.

COMPUTER, KEYBOARD

Fingers of palm down hands wiggle. Also means **TYPE**. May be combined with previous sign, or sign for **SCREEN**.

CONCENTRATE, FOCUS

Flat hands at sides of head move forward/down and twist in from wrists.

CONFIDENCE, CONFIDENT

'C' hand taps the chest twice.

CONFIDENCE (gain)

'C' hand moves upwards firmly on the chest. Also means **BE CONFIDENT.**

CONFIDENCE (lose)

'C' hand makes downward movement on the chest, the shoulders slump slightly.

CONFLICT, OPPOSE

Indexes pointing in make alternate short up and down movements. Movement may also be from side to side.

CONFUSED, CONFUSION

Open hands move in alternate small circles palm back in front of face. If body sways slightly, also means **DIZZY, FAINT.**

CONGRATULATIONS

Closed hands with thumbs up move in alternate forward circles towards the person/s concerned.

CONTACT, LINK, JOIN

Hands move towards each other and fingers of 'O' hands interlock. Also means **CONNECT.**

CONTINUE, CARRY ON

Palm down 'C' hands (or just one hand) move simultaneously to the right, or forwards. Also means **PERMANENT.**

CONTROL/LER, MANAGE/R

Palm facing Irish 'T' hands move alternately backwards and forwards. Also means **ADMINISTER, DEAL WITH, RUN**.

CONVERSATION, DISCUSS

Palm up flat hands move backwards and forwards alternately several times. Also means **CORRESPOND**.

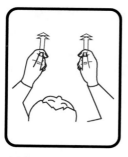

COOK, COOKER/Y, FEED

Palm facing Irish 'T' hands make two short movements forwards.

COOK, COOKERY, WHISK

Irish 'T' hand makes whisking movements in crook of left arm.
Varies.

COPY

Thumb of R. bent hand closes onto fingers as hand moves backwards from L. palm.

CORNER

Flat hands held at an angle tap fingertips together twice.

CORRECT, ACCURATE

Closed hand with thumb out makes circular movement then moves down onto L. palm. Also means **PROPER, RIGHT.**

CORRIDOR, HALL

'N' hands move forward at sides of head. Flat hands can be used. Also means **PASSAGE.**

COUGH

Index finger edge of fist bangs on chest twice.

COUNTRY

Palm down clawed hand moves round in small horizontal circles, may end with downward movement. *Varies.*

COUNTY COUNCIL

'C' hand makes a short move forward, then repeats slightly to the right. Also means **COCA-COLA**.

COURSE, SCHEME

Edge of R 'C' hand moves forward along L. hand.

COURT, TRIAL, TRIBUNAL

'N' hands move alternately up and down. Can be palm up or palm down or use flat hands. Also means **ASSESS/MENT**.

COURTING, GO OUT WITH

'N' hands move round together in small circles.

COUSIN

'C' hand makes short repeated forward movement. *Varies.*

COW

Thumb tips of 'Y' hands touch sides of head and twist upwards from palm down to palm forward.

CRASH, BUMP INTO, HIT

Knuckles of R. fist bang into L. palm. Cheeks may be puffed.

CREAM, ANTISEPTIC, RUB

Flat hand rubs in small circles on back of wrist, or on relevant part of body.

CREAM, CREAMY

Little finger strokes left to right across the chin. *Varies.*

CRISPS, CHIPS

R. 'O' hand moves repeatedly up to mouth from L. palm. Bunched hand may be used.

CRITICISE, CRITICISM

Closed hands with little fingers extended make alternate forward circles towards referent (*directional*), brows furrowed.

CRUEL, MEAN, SPITEFUL

Index twists into neck with menacing expression. Also means **KILL, VINDICTIVE.**

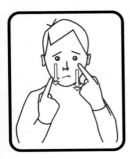

CRY, TEARS, WEEP

Index fingers move down cheeks under eyes alternately. One hand may be used. May *vary*.

CSW

COMMUNICATION SUPPORT WORKER
Fingerspell 'CSW' or combine the three signs together.

CUDDLE, EMBRACE, HUG

Closed hands are crossed on chest as body rocks slightly.

CULTURE, BELONG TO

R. closed hand bounces down onto L. palm, then forward twisting to palm forward.

CUPBOARD

Closed hand moves backwards in action of opening cupboard door. Both hands may be used.

CURRICULUM

R' full 'C' hand moves down L. hand and forearm in small hops. Also means **CONSTITUTION**.

CURTAINS

Irish 'T' hands move in action of closing or opening curtains.

CUT, CUT THROUGH

Fingers open and close several times as hand moves forward. Can be just single movement.

CUT (self), WOUND

Tip of index finger is drawn across back of left forearm, or on relevant part of the body.

CV, CURRICULUM VITAE

Fingerspell 'CV'.

DADDY, DAD, DAUGHTER

Repeat fingerspelt 'DD'. See also **FATHER**.

DANCE, DANCING

'V' hands (or 'N' hands) flick down from wrists in side-to-side movements. Head tilts right then left.

DANGER, DANGEROUS

Edge of R. flat hand comes up sharply to forehead. May tap twice on forehead.

DARK, DARKNESS, NIGHT

Palm back hands swing in/down to finish crossed. *Varies.*

DATE, ADDRESS

Closed hand taps side of chin twice. *Regional.*

DAY, DAWN, LIGHT

Palm back open hands start crossed and swing upwards and apart. **DAY** may be fingerspelt.

DEA

DISABILITY EMPLOYMENT ADVISER

Sign the three signs, or fingerspell 'DEA'.

DEAD, DEATH, DIE, DYING

'N' hands held apart and pointing forward twist down abruptly from wrists. Slow movement for **DYING.**

DEAF CLUB

'N' hand contacts ear, then moves forward as fingers curl into 'C' shape. **CLUB** is also often a fingerspelt contraction. **Varies.**

DEAF, DEAF PERSON

'N' hand contacts ear. Cheeks may be puffed for **PROFOUNDLY DEAF, REALLY DEAF.**

DEAFENED, BECOME DEAF

Bent hand with thumb out near ear moves down slightly as thumb closes onto fingers. Also means **LOSE HEARING.**

DECIDE, DEFINITE

Edge of R. index finger lands sharply on L. palm. *Varies.*

DEER, REINDEER

Thumbs of open hands on sides of head; hands move slightly forward and apart.

DELIGHT, JUMP FOR JOY

R. 'V' hand (legs classifier) stands on L. palm then jumps up flexing, may repeat several times with appropriate expression.

DENMARK, DANISH

Closed hand with thumb, index and middle finger extended moves left to right across chest in up and down movement.

DENTIST, EXTRACTION

Irish 'T' hand jerks forward/down from mouth, or index finger taps teeth twice.

DETERMINED

Palm left bent R. index twists firmly from wrist to finish palm back with tip touching chin, lips stretched.

DICTIONARY

R. 'C' hand forms a fingerspelt 'D' and makes repeated circles against L. index.

DIFFERENT, DIFFERENCE

Index fingers held together twist over and apart.

DIFFICULT, HARD

Tip of R. thumb prods into
L. palm twice.

DIGITAL

Fingers form fingerspelt 'D'
then R. hand moves to the
right as index finger opens
and closes onto thumb
several times.

DINNER LADY/NANNY

Sign for **DINNER** followed
by extended R. index
finger brushing forward on
cheek twice.

DINNER, RESTAURANT

'N' hands move up and down to the mouth alternately.   Also means **MEAL**.

DIRTY, GRIMY, MUCKY

Open hands rub together in anticlockwise circles (or closed hands rub at wrists) with appropriate facial expression. *Varies.*

DISABILITY, DISABLED

Hands form fingerspelt 'D' then R. index brushes down along the tips of L. fingers.

DISAGREE, DON'T AGREE

Closed hands with thumbs up touch at knuckles, then spring open and apart as the head shakes.

DISAPPOINT/MENT

Tips of 'V' hand prod neck, may repeat. Lips pressed together and turned down. Also **FRUSTRATED, MISS** (*regional*).

DISCRIMINATE, OPPRESS

R. open hand behind L. index pushes L. hand forcefully forward/down. *Directional.*

DIVORCE/D, SPLIT UP

Tips of index fingers touching, then hands swing forward/apart sharply from wrists.

DIZZY, SPIN, VERTIGO

The hand moves in small circles at side of head, twisting from the wrist. Also one version of **DRUNK.**

DLA

DISABILITY LIVING ALLOWANCE

Sign the meaning of each word, or fingerspell 'DLA'

DOCTOR, MEDICAL

Tips of R. hand middle finger (or index, or both) and thumb grasp left wrist. May tap twice. *Varies*

DOCTOR, MEDICAL

Tips of 'O' hand contact right, then left sides of chest. *Varies.*

DOG

'N' hands are held like a dog begging, with two short downward movements. *Varies.*

131

DON'T BELIEVE

Index to forehead then edge of flat hand lands on L. palm and brushes firmly away as head shakes.

DON'T KNOW

Flat hand swings down to palm up from forehead as shoulders shrug, head shakes, lips pressed together.

DON'T LIKE, DISLIKE

Open hand on chest twists forwards/up as head shakes with negative expression. May move palm down away from body.

DON'T TOUCH

Head shakes firmly as flat hands begin crossed and swing sharply apart, then R. hand moves slightly forward.

DON'T UNDERSTAND

Index fingers flick backwards over the shoulders. Often with lip-pattern 'pow' or 'whoosh'. Also means **OVER ONE'S HEAD.**

DON'T WANT, DON'T NEED

Flat hand moves firmly down and away from body as head shakes.

DONATE, FUND/ING

R. full 'C' hand moves in forward arc off L. palm, or in **direction** relevant to context. Also means **SPONSOR.**

DOOR, GATE

R. hand pivots forwards and back from wrist in front of L. May **vary** in context.

DOORBELL

Thumb moves forward in action of pressing a doorbell.

DOWN, SOUTH

Index finger points down and makes small downward movement. Also means **THIS, HERE, DOWNSTAIRS** (may repeat).

DRAMA, PERFORMANCE

Closed hands (or 'O' hands) with palms facing in/forward move alternately backwards and forwards on the chest.

DRAW, SKETCH

Palm back 'N' hand moves down in wiggling movements in front of face.

DRAWER, DRAWERS

Palm up closed hands move backwards together in action of opening drawer, move down and repeat for plural.

DREAM/Y, FANTASISE

Flat hand moves out in small circling movements from side of head, eyes may close. Also one version of IMAGINE.

DRESS, FROCK, WEAR

Open hands brush down chest and apart finishing palm down.

DRINK, BEER, GLASS

Full 'C' hand moves to mouth with small backward tipping movement. Can also be used for **JUICE, WATER.**

DRIVE, MOTOR

Palm back closed hands make firm movement forward together. May change in context.

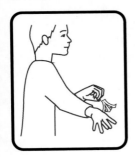

DROP, ABANDON

Palm down full 'O' hand moves down slightly as it springs open. Two hands may be used.

DROP OUT, PULL OUT OF

Fingers of R. bent 'V' hand pull backwards and away from L. bent hand. *Varies.*

DRUNK, TIPSY

Bent fingers of R. bent 'V' hand represent legs resting on L. palm as R. hand as rotates. *Varies.*

DRY, DRY OUT, DRIED

Thumbs rub across the fingertips from little fingers to indexes. One hand can be used.

DUCK, GOOSE

Fingers of bent hand (or 'N' hand) open and close onto thumb several times, in front of chin.

DURHAM

Palm forward bent 'V' hands (or closed hands), one higher than the other, make short repeated movements forward.

DUTY, RESPONSIBILITY

Bent hand taps shoulder twice. Both hands can be used.

E-MAIL

Index fingers flick off thumbs towards each other. Can be one hand only. ***Directional.***

EARLIER, EARLY, BEFORE

Edge of R. hand moves backward up L. arm in small arc. Also means **PREVIOUS, PRECEDE.** ***Varies.***

EARLY, EMERGENCY

R. index bangs sharply on L. index and bounces up again. Also means **QUICK, SUDDEN, URGENT.**

EASTER

R. thumb (or index finger) makes a cross on the back of L. hand. *Varies.*

EASY, SIMPLE, SOFT

Index finger prods into the cheek twice. The cheeks may be puffed.

EAT, FOOD

Bunched hand makes two short movements to the mouth.

141

EDUCATION, TEACH/ER

Bunched hands move from temples to point forward with two small movements. *Directional.*

EGG (boiled)

Palm up R. 'N' hand (or bent index) makes slicing movement across top of L. fist.

EGG, BREAK AN EGG

Palm facing clawed hands twist to palm down in action of breaking open an egg.

ELECTRIC, ELECTRICITY

Tips of bent 'V' hand tap the chin twice. Also means **BATTERY.** Or palm forward extended index moves down in small zig-zag. *Varies.*

ELEPHANT

Full 'C' hand moves down forward and up in outline of elephant's trunk.

END/ING, FINAL, LAST

Edge of R. flat hand lands sharply on extended L. little finger. R. hand can also be palm up or down.

ENGAGED, FIANCE/E

Tip of bent R. index finger twists over to contact back of L. ring finger.

ENGLAND, ENGLISH

R. index finger rubs up and down along the length of L. index finger.

ENJOY, PLEASURE

Hands make repeated contact brushing against each other with pleased expression. Also means **HAPPY, PLEASED.**

ENOUGH, SUFFICIENT

Bent hand brushes upwards/forwards twice under the chin. Also means **PLENTY**.

ENTER, ENTRY, GO IN

R. bent hand moves forward under palm down L. flat hand. Also a *regional* sign for **VISIT**.

EQUAL/ITY, FAIR

Palm down flat hands move apart, or hands may move alternately up and down. *Varies.*

145

EQUIPMENT, MACHINERY

Palm back clawed hands pointing up, swing down/in towards each other so that fingers intermesh.

ESCAPE, RUN OFF

R. index finger moves sharply forward under L. hand. Also means **ABSCOND**.

EUROPE

Fingertips bunched behind the thumb; hand moves in small anticlockwise circle.

EVENING, NIGHT, TONIGHT

Palm back flat hands swing in/down to finish crossed. *Varies.*

EVERY WEEK, WEEKLY

Hand in number 7 handshape makes repeated short forward movements from the cheek. *Varies.*

EVERY WEEK, WEEKLY

Extended index finger makes repeated movement along left forearm. *Varies.*

EVERY YEAR, YEARLY

Index fingers pointing towards each other; R. index finger makes several forward circles around L. Also means **ANNUALLY**.

EVERYDAY, DAILY

Backs of fingers are brushed forward across the cheek.

EVERYONE, EVERYTHING

Flat hand sweeps sideways.

EXAM, TEST

Closed hands held together at an angle twist round to change places, or index edge of R. 'N' hand rubs on L. palm. *Varies.*

EXCHANGE, SWAP

Palm up flat hands swap places with each other (*directional*). Handshape may *vary* in context eg Irish 'T' or 'O' or full 'C' hands.

EXCITED, EAGER, KEEN

Tips of clawed hands rub alternately up and down on chest with excited expression.

EXCUSE, FORGIVE

Tips of R. hand contact lips, then make small repeated rubbing movements on L. palm.

EXPENSIVE, DEAR

R. open hand taps fingertips on L. palm, then moves away to the right, shaking from the wrist, cheeks puffed.

EXPERIENCE

Thumb tip touches forehead then moves down as flat hand with fingertips brushing past L. palm. Also means **KNOW ABOUT**. *Varies.*

EXPLAIN, TELL ABOUT

Flat hands rotate round each other in forward circles eg '*I'll explain*' or backwards eg '*explain to me*'. ***Directional***.

EXTRA, ADD TO, INCREASE

Fingers of R. bent hand make tipping motion into L. palm. May repeat.

EYE CONTACT

Extended fingers of 'V' hands point towards each other. ***Directional***.

FACTORY, COMPANY, FIRM

Closed hands with thumbs up start together one behind the other, and move apart diagonally.

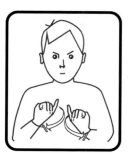

FAIL, FAILURE, SPOIL

Extended little fingers twist sharply to brush past each other and point down. Can be one hand only.

FALL, FALL DOWN/OVER

R. 'V' hand (legs classifier) stands on L. palm then twists to land palm up, or other movement to suit context.

FALSE, FAKE, NOT REAL

Tip of extended middle finger touches nose, then moves and twists to point forward. Also means **ARTIFICIAL, PRETEND.**

FAMILY

Open hand moves round in horizontal circle. *Varies*.

FAMILY

Hands form fingerspelt 'F' formation and move round in horizontal circle. *Varies*.

FANTASTIC, BRILLIANT

R. closed hand with thumb up bangs on L. palm and bounces up again with lip-pattern 'vee'.

FAR, LONG WAY, DISTANT

'L' hand makes small quick circling movement then makes large forward arc, cheeks puffed.

FARM, FARMER

Closed hand with thumb out moves from chest in forward arc to recontact the body. Also means **PAUNCH**.

FAST, IMMEDIATE

R. index bangs sharply on L. and bounces back up again. Also means **AUTOMATIC.**

FAT, CHUBBY, LARGE

Palm back open hands move apart with emphasis as cheeks puff out. Also signed with palm down closed hands, thumbs out.

FATHER, DAD/DY

Fingers form fingerspelt 'F' and tap twice. Also *regional* FRIDAY.

FAVOURITE, APPROVE

Palm down closed hands with thumbs out make two short movements down. *Varies.*

FAX, SEND A FAX

R. flat hand moves down/forward in small arc under L. or twists round and moves back to signer *(directional)*.

FED UP, SICK OF, ENOUGH

Bent hand bangs up against underside of chin. May repeat. Shoulders and corners of mouth droop.

FEED

Tips of bunched hands move forward/down from mouth in **direction** to suit context. **Varies.**

FEEL, EMOTION, SENSE

Tips of middle fingers brush upwards on chest. One hand can be used.

FEW

Tips of 'O' hand make repeated short brushing movements down the chin.

FEW, NOT MUCH

Thumb flicks up off index as hand twists down from wrist, eyes narrowed, shoulders raised.

FIGHT, CONFLICT, SCRAP

Extended little fingers bang up and down against each other, or move in to contact each other several times.

FILL IN FORM, NOTES

Tips of bent 'V' hand (or 'N' hand) make short movements towards L. palm several times, moving down.

FIND, DISCOVER

Index points to eye, then moves away closing sharply to a fist in upward grasping movement.

FINE, PENALTY, PUNISH

R. Irish 'T' hand (or index finger) moves sharply down across L. palm.

FINGERSPELL, SPELL

Fingers and thumbs wiggle against each other as hands move to the right. Refers to two handed fingerspelling.

FINISH, END, STOP

Fingers of bent hands close onto thumbs in short firm downward movement.

FINISH/ED, COMPLETED

Middle fingers close onto thumbs in quick repeated movements.
Regional.

FINISH/ED, COMPLETED

Closed hands with thumbs up and pointing slightly out move in outward circles.
Regional.

FIRE, BURN, FLAMES

Hands move up and down alternately with fingers flickering. Hands can be held palms facing.

FIRST, INITIAL/LY

R. flat hand strikes inside of L. thumb, or palm forward index moves upwards twisting to palm back. *Varies.*

FISH

Hand held with thumb on chin as fingers wiggle. Often used in referring to fishing ports and villages eg *regional* WHITBY.

FISH AND CHIPS

Thumb on chin as fingers wiggle, then full 'C' hand makes shaking movements above L. palm.

FISH, SWIM

Flat hand moves diagonally forward with quick wiggling movements from the wrist.

FLASHING DOORBELL

Thumb makes short forward movement then hand moves to head height springing open/down from full 'O' hand.

FLAT, APARTMENT

Palm down flat hands (or 'N' hands) move apart.

FLOOD, RISING WATER

Open hands move up simultaneously. Cheeks may be puffed.

FLOWER

'O' hand (or bunched or closed hand) moves from side to side under the nose as if sniffing a flower. Also **GARDEN** (*regional*).

FOG/GY, MIST, HAZE

Palm forward open hands move down and cross over in front of face, eyes slightly squinted.

FOLLOW, SHADOW

Upright index fingers, representing people, one in front of the other; both move forwards in front of the body.

FOLLOW, TAIL-GATE

Palm down flat hands, representing vehicles, one in front of the other; both move forwards in front of the body.

FOOTBALL, GAME, MATCH

Fingers of open hands bent slightly inwards; hand make short movements towards each other. *Varies.*

FOOTBALL, KICK A BALL

Index fingers held pointing down; R. hand twists forwards from wrist past the L. *Varies.*

FORBID, FORBIDDEN

Fists (or flat hands) start crossed and move firmly apart. Head may shake. Also means **NOT ALLOWED, TABOO.**

FORCE, COMPEL, REPRESS

R. open hand behind L. index pushes L. hand forcefully forward/down. *Directional.*

FORGET, FORGETFUL

Tips of bunched hand on forehead; hand springs open in forward movement. May *vary.*

FRANCE, FRENCH

Palm forward 'O' hand (or both hands) twists to palm back with slight movement out from side of face.

FREE, FREEDOM

Thumbs of open hands on upper chest, brush upwards, forwards and twist over to palm up.

FREE, GRATIS

R. hand of fingerspelt 'F' formation brushes forwards off back of L. twice.

FREEZE, FREEZER, FROZEN

Palm down open hands held out in front of body, move back flexing to clawed hands.

FRIEND, MATE, PAL

Hands clasp together and shake forward/down several times. *Varies.*

FRIGHTENED, FEAR

Tips of clawed hand (or both hands) tap chest twice as body cringes back.

FROM

R. flat hand makes short downward movement past L. palm.

FRUIT

Bent 'V' hand and thumb make repeated forward circular movements near the mouth. May **vary**.

FULL, FULL UP, FILL

R. bent hand moves up to contact underside of L. bent hand. May **vary** in context.

FUNNY, FUN, AMUSING

'C' hand near chin makes small side to side shaking movements, or both hands one above other in alternate movements.

FUNNY, PECULIAR, ODD

Index finger flicks out brushing across the chin. The nose is wrinkled and brows furrowed.

GAME, PLAY, PLAY ABOUT

Hands move up and down alternately several times, so that palms brush together. *Varies.*

GARAGE

GAME, GEOGRAPHY, GOVERNMENT, GUILTY, GREEN
Fingerspell 'GG'. These signs have other *variations.*

GARDEN, DIG

Palm up flat hand flips over to palm down several times. *Varies.*

GAY, HOMOSEXUAL

R. closed hand with thumb up rests on L. palm and makes small waggling movements from the wrist.

GERMAN, GERMANY

Side of hand with index finger extended taps front of forehead twice, or makes single contact.

171

GET, ACHIEVE, ADOPT

Palm left R. clawed hand moves in sharply closing to a fist.

GHOST, HAUNT, SPOOK

Open hands held loosely and shaking from wrists at sides of head.

GIRAFFE

Full 'C' hand moves upwards in front of neck and face.

GIRL, GIRLFRIEND

Edge of palm forward extended index finger brushes forward twice on cheek.

GIVE, OFFER, LET

Hands (or just one) move forward or in *direction* to suit context. Hanshape may also *vary*. Also means GIFT, PRESENT.

GLASGOW

Fingerspell 'G', then R. hand changes to open hand and bangs against L. fist.

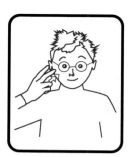

GLASSES, SPECTACLES

Middle fingertip of 'V' hand taps the upper cheek twice. Also means **OPTICIAN.**

GLOVE, PUT ON A GLOVE

R. hand grasps L. and moves down in action of pulling a glove on. Repeat L. on R. for plural.

GO, GONE, WENT

Flat hand moves forward in small arc. *Varies.*

GO, GONE, WENT, SENT

Index finger swings forward/up from wrist to point forward. *Varies.*

GOAT

Full 'C' hand moves forward with grasping movement from chin, closing to a fist. *Varies.*

GOD

Extended R. index finger twists sharply up/back from the wrist at side of head, with eye gaze.

GOING TO, INTEND

Back of extended thumb taps side of upper chest twice. Lips are stretched. Also means **ANTICIPATE, EXPECT**.

GOLD, GOLDEN

Hands form fingerspelt 'G' then spring open and apart.

GOOD, GREAT, HELLO

Closed hand (or both hands) with thumb up makes short movement forward.

GOOD LUCK, LUCK/Y

Thumb tip of 'L' hand brushes down from nose as hand twists to palm down. *Varies*.

GOOD NIGHT

R. extended thumb held up, then flat hands swivel down/in to cross each other in front of the face.

GOVERNMENT

Clawed hand on side of head makes short abrupt movement sideways/up, or fingerspell 'GG' or 'GOV'.

GRANDFATHER, GRANDAD

Fingerspell 'GF', or 'GD'.
The 'F' and 'D' may
repeat.

GRANDMOTHER, GRANDMA

Fingerspell 'GMM', or 'GM'
respectively.

GRASS, VEGETATION

Fingers of R. hand wiggle
as they move along behind
left forearm.

GREECE, GREEK

Palm back bunched hands make small repeated movements forwards and back.

GREED, GREEDY, SELFISH

Fist moves round in small circles in front of nose or chin. The nose is wrinkled.

GREEN, FIELD, GRASS

R. flat hand sweeps up left forearm. **Colours can vary widely.**

GREY

R. fist rubs in circular movement on L. (little fingers may be extended). **Colours can vary widely.**

GROUP, TEAM

Palm forward closed hands twist round in circle to finish palm back. Clawed hands or upright fingers may also be used. *Varies*.

GROUP, TEAM

Full 'C' hands move in twisting at the wrists to touch together at fingertips. *Varies*.

GROW UP, GROW

Palm down flat hand moves upwards.

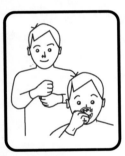

GUINEA PIG

Fingerspell 'G', then fist makes circling movements in front of the nose.

GYM, WORK OUT, PE

Fingertips of bent hands move up and down on shoulders several times. Also means **AEROBICS**.

HALF, PART

Edge of R. flat hand slices down across L. palm or front of body, or R. index slices down across L. index. *Varies.*

HALL, ALLEY, LOBBY

Flat hands pointing up move forward from near head. 'N' hands can be used.

HAMMER

Irish 'T' hand moves in action of holding and using a hammer.

HAMSTER

Clawed hands make small movements near sides of chin.

HAPPEN, ARISE, CROP UP

R. index moves sharply up behind L. hand, or makes upward flicking movement in front of L. hand.

HAPPY, ENJOY, GLAD

Hands make repeated contact brushing against each other, with pleased expression.

HARE

Palm back 'N' hands at sides of head twitch backwards several times.

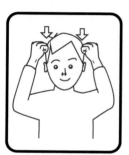

HAT

Hands move in action of placing a hat on the head. Handshape and movement will *vary*.

HAVE A LOOK, LET'S SEE

Tip of index finger taps cheek just below eye twice.   Also means **CHECK OUT**.

HAVE, GET, POSSESS/ION

Palm up clawed hand makes slight downward movement as it closes firmly.

HAVEN'T, NOTHING

Flat hand makes sharp brushing movement past the lips as air is blown through them.

HAVEN'T SEEN FOR AGES

'O' hands move from over right shoulder, forward/left, cheeks puffed.

HE, HER, HIM, IT, SHE

Index points with short movement towards referent. Sideways sweep for plurals. *Directional*.

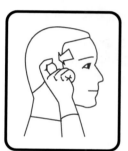

HEARING AID (post-aural)

Bent index finger touches side of head above ear. *Varies* in context.

HEARING (not deaf)

Index finger moves from ear to mouth. May finish with repeated tap on chin.

HEAVY, WEIGHTY

Palm up hands move down with stress (may repeat) shoulders sag, cheeks may be puffed.

HELLO, HI

Flat hand with thumb tucked in makes short movement out from near side of head. *Varies*.

HELP/ER, ASSISTANT

Closed hand with thumb up rests on L. palm as hands move forward together. Also means **SUPPORT**. *Directional.*

187

HER/S, HIS, ITS

Palm forward closed hand is directed towards referent. Sideways sweep for plurals. *Directional.*

HERE, THIS

Index finger makes two short downward movements. Two hands can be used. Also means **DOWNSTAIRS**.

HGV

Fingerspell 'HGV'.

HIDE

Flat hands move side to side across each other in front of face.

HIGH CHAIR

Bent hand makes upward movement followed by closed hands making short firm movement down.

HOLD, HANG ON TO

Fist makes short firm movement down. May change in context.

189

HOLIDAY

Flat hands move from sides of head, twisting to palm forward, slightly down and apart. *Varies*.

HOLIDAY, CELEBRATION

Irish 'T' hands make circling movements near sides of head, or same movement with extended middle fingers *(regional)*.

HOLY, SACRED

R. closed hand with thumb out circles above, then lands down onto L. palm.

HOME

Tips of flat hands touch, with hands held at an angle.

HONEST, GENUINE, REAL

Edge of R. flat hand lands sharply on L. palm. Mouth may be open and close with the movement as in eg **REALLY?**

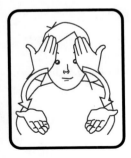

HONOUR, RESPECT, OBEY

Flat hands touch forehead, then swing forward and down to finish palm up.

HOOVER, VACUUM

Irish 'T' hand moves backwards and forwards several times.

HOPE, HOPEFULLY, WISH

Fingers are held crossed, palm forward. May be one hand only. *Varies*.

HORSE, PONY, RIDE

Palm down closed hands make repeated movements forward/down. *Varies*.

HOSPITAL

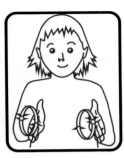

Palm facing flat hands make several simultaneous forward circling movements. *Regional*.

HOSPITAL

Palm back flat hands circle round each other. *Regional*.

HOSPITAL, AMBULANCE

R. thumb tip (or can be index fingertip) draws cross on left upper arm. Also one version of **NURSE**. *Varies*.

HOT CHOCOLATE

Clawed hand is drawn across mouth, then 'C' hand brushes downwards twice on chin.

HOT, HEAT, HEATING

Clawed hand is drawn sharply across the mouth. Can be flat hand drawn across forehead then shaken.

HOTEL, ACCOMMODATION

Flat hands (or 'C' hands) at sides of head move forward/down twisting to palm down.

HOUR

R. 'O' hand moves round in circle over left wrist or palm, or R. extended index twists round in full circle. **Varies**.

HOUSE, HOME

'N' hands at an angle, touch at fingertips then twist down/apart. Flat hands can also be used.

HOW?

Knuckles of clawed hands tap together twice, palm back or palm up, eyebrows raised or furrowed.

HOW ARE YOU?

Tips of bent hands on chest; hands move forward closing with thumbs up, eyebrows raised. Also means **ARE YOU WELL?**

HOW MANY? HOW MUCH?

Hand held palm back with fingers wiggling. Eyebrows are raised or furrowed.

HOW OLD? WHAT AGE?

Fingers wiggle in front of nose. Eyebrows are raised or furrowed.

HUNGRY

Open hand makes circular rubbing movements on stomach. *Varies.*

HURT, PAIN/FUL, SORE

Palm back open hands shake up and down from the wrists alternately in front of the body with pained expression.

HUSBAND, WIFE, SPOUSE

R. index finger (or middle finger) and thumb contact upper L. ring finger twice. Also means **WEDDING, RING**.

I, ME

Tip of extended index finger contacts the chest.

I'M WELL

Tips of bent hands touch chest, then hands move forward closing with thumbs up as head nods.

ICE, ICY, FROST/Y

Palm down clawed hands held out, move backwards.

ICE-CREAM, CORNET

Fist makes repeated downward brushing movements near mouth, tongue slightly out.

IDEA, NOTION

Index finger flicks up at side of head. *Varies*.

IGNORE, TAKE NO NOTICE

Index finger palm forward near ear, twists sharply down and away as head turns. Both hands may be used. *Directional.*

ILL, ILLNESS, NOT WELL

R. index finger touches forehead, then moves down and taps twice against L. extended index. *Varies.*

ILL, ILLNESS, NOT WELL

Little fingers (or just one) brush down chest, head may tilt, may repeat. Also means **TIRED.**

IMITATION, PRETEND

Tip of extended middle finger touches nose, then moves and twists to point forward. Also means **FAKE, MOCK.**

IMPORTANT, CRUCIAL

R. open hand comes down to land on tip of L. index. May tap twice. Also means **TOP**.

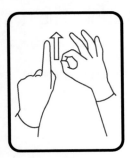

IMPROVE, GET BETTER

Tips of R. 'O' hand move upwards on upright L. index finger.

IN, GO IN, ENTER, ENTRY

R. bent hand straightens to a flat hand as it moves forward under L. hand.

INDIA, INDIAN

Index fingers move down and towards each other in jagged movement, or tip of index on forehead twists from palm left to palm back. *Varies.*

INFORM, INFORMATION

Index fingers make quick alternate movements backwards and forwards from the mouth.

INSURE, INSURANCE

Edge of R. bent hand moves diagonally down across the chest.

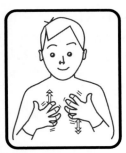

INTEREST, STIMULATE

Clawed hands rub up and down alternately on the body with animated expression.

INTERNET, NET, WEB

Tips of middle fingers touch briefly, then hands move out and round in sphere shape.

INTERPRET/ER

'V' hands (or 'N' hands) twist alternately backwards and forwards from the wrists.

INTERRUPT, INTERFERE

R. flat hand moves sharply through fingers of L. in forward movement or twists to move back to signer (*directional*). Also means **BUTT-IN**.

INTERVIEW, CONVERSE

Palm facing index fingers move forward and back to the mouth alternately. Also means **DIALOGUE, DISCUSS**.

IRELAND (N), IRISH

Tips of R. bent 'V' hand tap back of L. closed hand twice, or R. middle finger flicks off thumb twice on left shoulder.

IRON, IRONING, PRESS

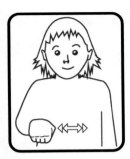

Closed hand moves in action of holding and using an iron with side to side movements.

ITALY, ITALIAN

Palm forward 'C' hand moves down with small side to side wavy movements. *Varies.*

JEALOUS/Y, ENVY

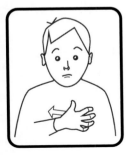

Tips of clawed hand are drawn across the chest, or edge of bent index finger taps the chin. *Varies.*

JEANS, BOTTOMS, PANTS

Fists pull upwards sharply at sides of waist.

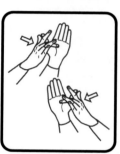

JESUS

Tip of R. middle finger prods into L. palm, then reverse L. into R.

JIGSAW PUZZLE

Thumbs make alternate repeated downward pressing movements, moving forwards.

JOINERY, CARPENTRY

Closed hands move in action of holding and using a plane with diagonal movements backwards and forwards.

JOKE, KID, HAVE ON

Palm down hands; R. brushes forwards on back of L. repeatedly in *direction* of referent. Can twist back to signer. *Varies.*

JOKE, KID, HAVE ON

Thumb tip of 'V hand brushes twice across tip of nose. *Regional.*

JUMP

R. 'V' hand (legs classifier) jumps up flexing on L. palm or in way to suit context. Repeated for **BABY BOUNCER, TRAMPOLINE.**

JUMPER, SWEATER

Closed hands touch upper, then lower chest.

JUST, ONLY JUST

Tips of 'O' hand move down cheek. Lips may be stretched, and eyebrows raised. Also means **A LITTLE WHILE AGO.**

KEEP FIT, EXERCISE

Fingertips of bent hands move up and down on shoulders several times.

KEEP, HANG ON TO

Palm to palm bent hands; R. taps L. hand twice.

KETCHUP, SAUCE

R. flat hand bangs against edge of L. full 'C' hand several times.

KETTLE

'Y' hand moves inwards in small arc. May *vary* to suit different models.

KEY, KEYS

Irish 'T' hand twists repeatedly from wrist. Firm clockwise turn for **LOCK**, anticlockwise for **UNLOCK**.

KICK, KICK OUT, SACK

R. index fingers twists sharply forward from wrist, brushing against tip of L. index finger. *Directional*.

KILL, MEAT

Index finger jabs into side of neck.

KISS

Tips of R. 'N' hand contact lips, then move down to contact tips of L. 'N' hand. *Varies.*

KISS

Tips of R. bunched hand contact lips, then move down to contact tips of L. bunched hand. *Varies.*

KITCHEN

Repeat fingerspelt initial

KNOW

Thumb tip taps on side of forehead.

LANGUAGE

Palm forward 'L' hands move apart. Hands may alternatively be palm back, pointing in. *Varies*.

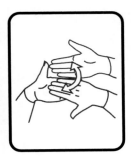

LAPTOP COMPUTER

Palm back flat hands, R. on top of L. twists over to contact L. palm, then back again.

LAST, FINAL, END

Edge of R. flat hand lands emphatically on extended L. little finger. *Varies.*

LATE, OVERDUE

R. extended index twists sharply forward/down across L. palm.

LAUGH/TER, FUNNY

'C' hands, one above the other, make alternate small side to side shaking movements under the chin. Also means **HUMOUR.**

LAW, RULE, PRINCIPLE

Edge of R. index finger lands sharply on L. palm.

LAZY, IDLE

R. bent hand taps left elbow twice, tip of tongue between teeth. Also one version of **BISCUIT.**

LEAGUE, RESULTS

Palm forward closed hands with thumbs out move up and down alternately.

LEARN, ACQUIRE, TAKE IN

Palm forward hand (or both hands) twists back to side of head, closing to a bunched hand. *Varies.*

LEAVE, GO, DEPART

Palm back flat hand swings forward/right from wrist to finish palm down.

LECTURE, GIVE SPEECH

Flat hand makes small repeated forward and backward movements at side of head.

LEND, LOAN, HIRE OUT

Closed hands held palm to palm and at an angle; hands move forward in small arc. *Directional.*

LESBIAN

R. 'L' hand rests on L. palm and makes small waggling movements from the wrist.

LET YOU KNOW

Bent hand with thumb out moves down from forehead and forward closing to a bunched hand, or onto chest (**LET ME KNOW**). *Directional.*

LETTER, MAIL, STAMP

Tip of extended thumb touches lips, then moves down to contact L. palm. Also *regional* **INSURANCE**.

LIE DOWN, LAY DOWN

R. 'V' hand (legs classifier) is drawn palm up across L. palm.

LIE, LIAR, FIB

R. index finger is drawn sharply to the right, brushing across the chin.

LIGHT (off), LIGHTS OUT

Open hand with fingers pointing down moves up slightly snapping shut. Can be both hands and *located* to suit context.

LIGHT (on), PUT LIGHT ON

Full 'O' hand springs down/open. Can be *located* to suit context, both hands for plural.

LIGHTNING, ELECTRIC/ITY

Palm forward index moves downward sharply in zigzag.

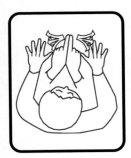

LIKE, SAME AS

Palm down hands with indexes extended and touching spring open and apart.

LIPREAD, LIP-PATTERN

Bent 'V' hand makes small circles in front of mouth. Can be palm forward, held forward (*directional*).

LIST, PROGRAMME

R. hand with thumb out moves down/back from L. palm with quick twisting movements from wrist.

LISTEN

Open hand moves to ear, closing to a bunched hand, or cupped hand held behind ear.

LITTLE, BIT, TINY

Index and thumb indicate small amount.

LIVE, ALIVE, LIFE

Tip of middle finger (or clawed hand) rubs up and down on side of chest.

LIVERPOOL

'L' hand pointing forward makes short quick twisting movements from the wrist. Also one version of **LESBIAN**.

LIVING-ROOM

Sign for **LIVE** followed by index fingers indicating outline shape, or flat hands indicating room shape (see **ROOM**).

221

LONDON, NOISE, NOISY

Index finger makes repeated forward circles near the ear.

LOOK AFTER, SUPERVISE

R. 'V' hand on top of L. at an angle; hands move down from near eye.

LOOK AROUND, SIGHTSEE

'V' hand (eye gaze classifier) moves right with small up and down movements or in **direction** to suit context.

LOOK, LOOK AT, WATCH

'V' hand (eyes classifier) makes short movement forward, or in **direction** to suit context.

LOSE, LOST, WASTE

Palm down full 'O' hands spring open and slightly apart.

LOUD, NOISY, RACKET

Index finger pointing to ear moves round in forward circles.

LOVE, ADORE, DEAR

Flat hands (or closed hands) are held crossed on the chest.

LOVELY, TASTY, DELICIOUS

R. thumb moves across chin from left to right.

LUCK/Y, GOOD LUCK

Thumb tip of 'L' hand brushes down from nose as hand twists to palm down. *Varies*.

MAKE, CREATE, FIX, MEND

Fingertips of bunched hands twist against each other several times.

MAKE, DO, REPAIR, MEND

Edge of R. fist bangs top of L. fist in circular movements.

MAN, MALE, BEARD

Fingers and thumb stroke down chin and thumb closes onto fingers. May repeat.

225

MANAGE, ORGANISE

Fingers brush backwards and forwards alternately against each other.

MANCHESTER

Hands form fingerspelt 'M' then form 'C' with index, middle and ring fingers. *Varies*.

MANY, LOADS, TOO MANY

Fingers of palm back hands wiggle as hands move apart, cheeks puffed.

MARRIED, WEDDING

R. flat hand brushes upwards along L. fingers, then circles back to land on back of L. hand.

MATCH, MATCHING

Tips of bent hands touch each other.

MAXIMUM, LIMIT, UP TO

R. fist moves up sharply to hit L. palm.

MAYBE, MIGHT, PERHAPS

'Y' hand waggles quickly from wrist, lips stretched.

MEAN, STINGY, TIGHT

Palm down hands move back to body as fingers flex tightly into clawed hands.

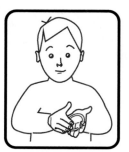

MEAN/ING CONTEXT

Fingers of R. flat hand rub in circles on L. palm.

MEAT, BEEF, BUTCHER

Index finger jabs into neck twice.

MEDICINE

R. Irish 'T' hand tips over above the L. which then moves up to the mouth. *Varies.*

MEDICINE

Extended R. little finger makes circular movements inside L. cupped hand. Also means **CHEMIST**.

MEET

Upright index fingers (person classifiers) held apart, move in towards each other. *Directional*.

MEETING, CONFERENCE

Index fingers circle round each other.

MIDDLE, MEDIUM

Edge of R. flat hand taps twice on top of L. middle finger.

MILES

Closed hands move backwards and forward to chest several times. *Varies*.

MILK

Hands move up and down alternately with squeezing actions, or closed hands rub against each other. *Varies*.

MILK

'Y' hands move up and down alternately. *Varies*.

MINE, MY, MY OWN

Closed hand moves back to contact chest. May repeat. Also means **BELONGS TO ME.**

MINICOM, TEXT PHONE

L. 'Y' hand held above palm down R. hand with wiggling fingers.

MIRROR, REFLECTION

Hand makes small quick repeated twisting movements in front of face, eye gaze is to the hand.

MISERABLE, MOODY

Clawed hand moves down in front of face (fingers may flex), brows furrowed, nose wrinkled and lips pressed together.

MISS, MISTAKE, WRONG

Index fingers move in sharply and brush past each other, lips are pressed together.

MISTAKE, ERROR, SORRY

Clawed hand makes small shaking movements near chin or side of head. *Varies*. Also means **ACCIDENT**.

MIX-UP, CONFUSE

Clawed hands circle round each other, tongue tip between teeth. Also means **COMPLEX, COMPLICATED.**

MONEY, CASH, FINANCE

Backs of fingers of R. bunched hand tap L. palm twice. *Varies*.

MONEY, CASH, FINANCE

Index edge of Irish 'T' hand taps L. palm twice. *Varies*.

MORE

R. flat hand moves back to tap back of L. twice or R. hand moves forward and away from L.

MORNING, GOOD MORNING

Fingertips of R. bent hand (with thumb up) touch left then right side of chest. *Varies*.

MOST/LY, MAJORITY

R. index brushes forward sharply against L.

MOTHER, MUM, MUMMY
Tips of 'M' hand tap side of forehead. *Regional.*

MOTHER, MUM, MUMMY
Form fingerspelt 'M' and tap twice.

MOUSE (computer)
Palm down hand with fingers curled moves in action of holding and moving a mouse.

MOUSE, MICE

Tip of index finger on side of nose; hand makes quick twisting movements from wrist. A single twist is *regional* sign for **PIG**.

MOVE, SHIFT

Palm facing flat hands move firmly sideways. Will *vary* in context.

MURDER

Tip of thumb is drawn sharply across the throat. *Varies.*

MUSIC, MUSICAL

'O' hands (or extended index fingers) swing in and out towards each other several times.

MYSELF, PERSONALLY

Extended index finger makes two short downward brushing movements on the chest.

NAME, CALLED

Tips of 'N' hand touch side of forehead, then move and twist forward.

NANA, NAN

Fingerspell 'N' and tap twice, or fingerspell whole word.

NAPPY

Fingers snap closed onto thumbs against sides of body, or flat hands cross over on the stomach or other *variation* in context.

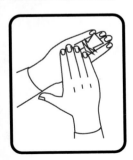

NAUGHTY, BOTHER

R. flat hand (or bent hand) taps back of L. twice, or sign for **BAD** with two short forward movements.

NEARLY, ALMOST

Tip of index and thumb pinched, hand moves slightly backwards and forwards, eyes narrowed, shoulders raised.

NEGATIVE

Edge of R. index finger bangs against palm forward L. hand.

NEIGHBOUR, NEXT-DOOR

Thumb tip contacts shoulder, then twists over to palm up. *Directional*.

NEPHEW, NIECE

Tips of 'N' hand tap twice on chin (also *regional* sign for **BOY**) or fingerspell 'NN'.

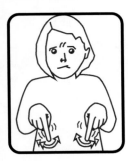

NERVOUS

Index fingers point down and make quick side to side shaking movements. Open hands can be used. *Varies*.

NETHERLANDS, DUTCH

Bent hands with thumbs out move up and out closing to bunched hands at sides of head. Also means **HOLLAND**.

NEVER

R. flat hand chops sharply down back of L. (L. can be flat hand or fist).

NEW, FRESH, LATEST

R. flat hand brushes sharply up behind L.

NEWCASTLE

Hands form fingerspelt 'N', then fingers and thumb form 'C' shape.

NEWSPAPER, MAGAZINE

Hands twist over and apart in action of holding and opening a newspaper. Also means **CATALOGUE.**

NEXT, AFTER, THEN, TURN

Extended thumb twists over from palm down to palm up. *Directional*.

NICE, SWEET, APPETISING

R. thumb moves across chin from left to right.

243

NIGHT, TONIGHT, DARK

Palm back flat hands swing in/down in front of face to finish crossed. *Varies.*

NO, DENY, REFUSE

R, closed hand (head classifier) twists emphatically to point forward as the head shakes.

NOISE, NOISY, SOUND

Index finger pointing to ear moves in forward circles.

NON-MANUAL FEATURES

Irish 'T' hands on cheeks move alternately up and down. (Refers to face and body language in BSL grammar).

NORMAL, NATURAL

Fingerspell 'N' and tap twice or brush forward along L. palm twice.

NORWAY, NORWEGIAN

'N' hand moves up and down in N shape in front of body.

NOT BOTHERED

R. bent hand taps back of L. hand, then moves away twisting over to palm up, with a shrug. Also means **DOESN'T MATTER.**

NOT, DON'T, FORBIDDEN

Flat hands start crossed, then swing emphatically apart as the head shakes. Also means **NOT ALLOWED.**

NOT SURE, UNCERTAIN

R. flat hand on L. palm makes wavering waggling movements, lips are pressed together.

NOT YET, BEFORE, WAIT

Palm forward closed hands make short repeated movements in towards each other as head shakes with 'shh' lip-pattern.

NOTHING, NONE, NOBODY

'O' hands (or full 'O' hands) shake from side to side, or make repeated circles towards each other. Tongue tip may protrude.

NOW, AT PRESENT

Palm up flat hands make two short movements down.   Single firm movement for **RIGHT NOW**.

247

NUMBER, DATE, MATHS

Knuckles of closed hand tap chin twice.

NURSE

Tips of 'C' hand are drawn across the forehead. *Varies*.

NURSERY

Tip of extended middle finger brushes down chin twice. *Regional. Varies.*

OBJECT, HATE, REJECT

Edge of extended R. little finger sweeps forward along L. palm, brows are furrowed. *Directional*.

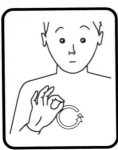

OFFICE

Palm forward 'O' hand moves round in small circles. *Varies.*

OFFICE, SECRETARY

'O' hand moves along L. palm with small squiggling movements. *Varies.*

OLD, AGED, ELDERLY

Fingers of ' 'V' hand flex as hand moves down in front of nose. Also *regional* DARK, NIGHT.

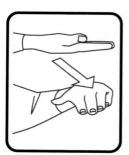

ON (physically), PUT ON

Back of R. flat hand is placed on back of L.

ONE TO ONE, FACING

Extended index fingers (person classifiers) face each other with short movement down. Can be located to suit context.

ONION, CRY, TEARS

Index finger brushes downwards under eye with quick twisting movements from the wrist.

ONLY, ONLY ONE, ALONE

R. index finger moves down and to the right behind L. hand.

OPEN, LAUNCH

Palm back flat hands swing open and apart. *Varies* in context.

OPPOSITE

Index fingers pointing towards each other (or may be upright) move apart in small arcs. *Directional*.

ORAL, ORALISM

Bent 'V' hand moves in small circles near mouth.

ORANGE (fruit and colour)

Clawed hand makes repeated squeezing movements near side of mouth. **Colours can vary widely.**

ORDER, CALL FOR

Hand bends sharply down from wrist while moving down and to the left.   Also means **SUMMON**.

ORDER, SEQUENCE, TURN

Thumb twists over repeatedly as it moves to the right. Also means **SERIES**. *Varies.*

ORGANISE,ORGANISATION

Middle fingertip of R. 'V' hand contacts L. palm, then twists and contacts with index fingertip and repeats.

OTHERS, ETC, SEVERAL

R. index swivels round from wrist brushing down L. fingertips. Also means **AND SO ON, THE REST.**

OUR/S, BELONG TO US

Palm forward closed hand (or both hands moving apart) sweeps round to end palm back on the chest. Also means **OUR OWN.**

OUTSIDE, ABROAD

Bent hand makes two short forward movements. Also means **FOREIGN/ER.**

OVEN, GRILL, ROAST

Palm up R. flat hand moves forward under L. palm down hand.

OVER, GO OVER

R. bent hand moves over L. hand in small arc.

OVERCAST, DULL

Bent hands move inwards to cross over each other over the head.

OWE

R. 'O' hand moves forward in small arc from L. palm. *Varies.*

PAGER (vibrating)

Fingers vibrate rapidly against thumb near waist.

PAIN, HEART ATTACK

Index fingers make two short jabs towards each other on appropriate part of body eg near head for **HEADACHE**.

PAINT, PAINTING

'N' hand (or flat hand) sweeps up and down in brushing movements.

PARENT/S

Hands form fingerspelt 'M', then fingerspelt 'F' **MOTHER/FATHER.**

PARK, GREEN

Edge of R. flat hand taps left upper chest twice.

PARK, STATIONARY (car)

Edge of R. flat hand rests on L. palm; hands make short movement down.

PARK, SWINGS

Closed hands swing backwards and forwards several times.

PARTIALLY DEAF

R. flat hand is drawn down across L. palm, then 'N' hand touches ear.

PARTNER, MATE, FRIEND

Knuckles of closed hands with thumbs up tap together twice. **Varies.**

PARTY, HAVE FUN, SOCIAL

'Y' hands twist repeatedly from wrists as arms move in circular waving movements. Cheeks may be puffed.

PARTY, TEA PARTY

'O' hands move up and down to the mouth alternately.

PASS

R. flat hand with thumb tucked in twists down past L. palm. Also a regional sign for **ABOUT** and **DECIDE**. *Varies.*

PASTA

Palm up 'V' hands move upwards. May repeat.

PATIENCE, TOLERANCE

Flat hands brush alternately down the body, lips pressed together. Also means **CALM**.

PAY, PAYMENT, PAY FOR

R. bunched hand (or Irish T hand) moves forward from L. palm in small arc. ***Directional***.

PEACE, QUIET, CALM

'O' hands touch, then swing slightly down and apart slowly.

PEAR

R. 'N' hand makes soft brushing movements, twisting from palm left to palm back at side of mouth.

PEOPLE

Palm forward index finger moves down in short zigzag or index finger, palm left with little finger up, taps chin twice. *Regional*.

PEOPLE, HUMAN, PUBLIC

Index and thumb close together as they brush down chin, then index finger brushes forward on cheek.

PERCENT, PERCENTAGE

Full 'O' hand moves diagonally right, then down. 'O' hand can also be used.

PERFECT, EXCELLENT

Palm forward 'O' hand makes two short movements forward, lips pressed together. Both hands can be used.

PERSON, INDIVIDUAL

Palm forward 'C' hand moves down. Also means **STUDENT**.

PETROL, GARAGE

'L' hand moves down twisting downwards from the wrist.

PICK UP, CATCH

Palm forward hands move back to body as fingers close onto thumbs (eg *catch flu*), or to the head (eg *pick up facts*).

PICNIC, BUFFET

Bunched hands move alternately up and down to the mouth. *Varies.*

PICTURE, NOTICE, PAPER

Index fingers move out down and back together in outline shape. Also means **CHART, DIAGRAM.**

PIE, PIZZA, PLATE

R. index finger pointing down circles round above L. palm.

PIG, PORK

Fist moves round in small circles in front of nose.

PINK

Palm left R. index (little finger may also be extended) moves down in front of nose. **Colours can vary widely.**

PIPE, CABLE, TUBE

'O' hands (or full 'O' hands) move apart.

PLACE, TOWN, BUILDING

Palm down clawed hand makes short movement down.

PLAN, DESIGN, DEVISE

Middle fingertip of R. 'V' hand contacts L. palm, then twists and contacts with index fingertip and repeats.

266

PLASTER, ELASTOPLAST

R. thumb moves across back of L. hand, or on appropriate part of the body.

PLATE

R. index finger pointing down makes small circles around L. palm.

PLAY, GAME

Palm up open hands move in simultaneous circular movements.

267

PLEASE, THANKS

Tips of flat hand touch mouth, then hand swings forward/down to finish palm up.

PLEASED, HAPPY, GLAD

Flat hand rubs in circles on chest with pleased expression.

PLUG, PLUG IN

Index, middle and ring fingers extended and bent; hand makes short movement forward.

POLICE

Fingers of R. 'V' hand flex as hand is drawn across back of L. wrist.

POLICE STATION

Sign for **POLICE** followed by palm down closed hand making short movement down.

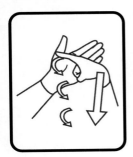

POLICY, RULES

R. index moves down/back from L. palm, or down left arm in small hops. Also means **PRINCIPLES**.

POO, SMELLY

Waft flat hand up and down in front of the nose, or grasp the nose with index finger and thumb.

POOR, SCRUFFY

R. clawed hand makes two scratching movements near left elbow.

POORLY, NOT WELL

R. flat hand is drawn across the forehead. *Varies.*

POPULAR, ADMIRE

Closed hands with thumbs up make alternative quick forward circling movements.

POSITIVE, PLUS

R. index taps twice against L. at right angles.

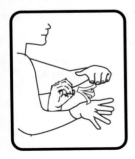

POST, MAIL, SEND

Full 'O' hand moves forward springing open under L. hand.

POST OFFICE

Edge of R. closed hand bangs on L. palm and then on fingers.

POSTER, NOTICE

Extended thumbs press forward at head height, and then move down and repeat lower down.

POSTPONE, DELAY

'O' hands move forward together in small arc. Also means, **PUT OFF.** The hands move back for **BRING FORWARD.**

POTATO, PEEL, PEELER

R. thumb moves over palm up L. full 'C' hand in action of holding and peeling a potato. *Varies*.

POTTY

R. index finger pointing down moves in circle above and to the right of L. fist.

PRIEST, CLERGY, VICAR

'C' hands pull apart in front of neck in outline of clerical collar. One hand may be used. Also *regional* sign for **PRESTON**.

PRINCE/ESS, ROYAL

Tips of clawed hand touch side of the head.

PRINT, PRINTER

R. closed hand twists over to contact L. palm and back again. *Varies.*

PRISON, PRISONER

R. closed hand moves down firmly to contact L. at the wrists at right angles.

274

PRIVATE, SECRET

Flat hands move in and out across each other in front of mouth. Also means **CONFIDENTIAL**, hands may grasp shut.

PROBLEM, DIFFICULTY

Tip of R. thumb prods into L. palm twice.

PROCESS, PROCEDURE

Palm down closed hands with thumbs out move forwards circling round each other. Bent hands may also be used.

PROFIT, BENEFIT, GAIN

Tips of 'O' hand twist over and brush down side of upper chest, may repeat.

PROGRAMME

R. open hand shakes repeatedly side to side on L. index finger. Hands may move down at same time.

PROMISE, SWEAR, TRUTH

R. index finger moves from mouth changing to flat hand banging edge down on L. palm.

PROOF, EVIDENCE

Index finger contacts face just under one eye then the other. Also means **WITNESS**

PROTECT, RESCUE, SAVE

R. bent hand on L. palm as hands move back to body.

PROTECT/ION, DEFEND

R. closed hand pushes forwards against L. index finger. Also means **PREVENT/ION**. *Varies*.

PROTESTANT

Edge of R. bent hand moves diagonally down across the chest

PROUD, PRIDE

Extended thumbs brush alternately down the chest in alternate backward circles.

PUB, BAR

R. closed hand held upright from elbow on L. hand makes short backward movement. Can be R. hand only. *Varies*.

PURPLE

R. index finger flicks open twice off thumb against end of L. index finger. **Colours can vary widely.**

PUSHCHAIR, BUGGY

Palm down fists move forward together. Also means **PRAM.**

QUALIFICATION/S

Hands form fingerspelt 'Q' and make short movement down. Also means **QUALITY.**

QUEASY, SICKLY

Clawed hand makes repeated circular movements on lower abdomen.

QUEEN, KING, CROWN

Tips of clawed hand touch side of head.

QUESTION, QUERY

Palm forward 'O' hand moves round in small circle, then makes short forward movement.

QUICK, FAST, HURRY

R. index taps on L. several times very quickly.

QUIET/LY, HUSH, SH

Index finger to lips, then 'O' hands touch, then swing slightly down and apart slowly.

RABBIT

Palm forward 'N' hands held at sides of head twitch forwards several times. Also one version of **HARE**.

281

RAIN, DRIZZLE

Open hands make two movements down, the fingers may wiggle slightly, or may move with force, cheeks puffed for **HEAVY RAIN**.

RAINBOW

Palm forward full 'C' hand moves over in large arc. Also means **ARCH, BRIDGE**.

READ

R. 'V' hand (eye gaze classifier) sweeps from side to side above L. palm. *Direction* and movement will suit context.

READY, PREPARED

Thumbs of open hands (or just one hand) tap upper chest twice, or make upward brushing movements. Also means **GET READY**.

REAL, FACT, DEFINITE

Edge of R. flat hand bangs sharply down on L. palm.

REALLY? SURPRISED

Tips of clawed hand tap chest twice as body leans slightly forward. Mouth may be slightly open, or turned down.

REASON, BECAUSE

Edge of R. index finger taps against left upper chest twice.

RECENTLY, JUST NOW

Fingers of R. flat hand bend backwards twice at side of face, lips stretched.

RED

Index finger flexes as it makes repeated small brushing movements near the lips. **Colours can vary widely.**

REDUNDANT, LAY OFF

Irish 'T' hand moves forward/down or in **direction** relevant to context.

REFUGEE, ESCAPEE

R. index finger moves sharply forward under L. hand. **Directional.**

REFUSE, DENY

R. closed hand (head classifier) twists firmly to point forward as the head shakes with emphasis.

RELATIONSHIP, RELATE

Fingers of 'O' hands interlock, and hands move backwards and forwards several times. Also **BOND, LIAISE, RAPPORT**.

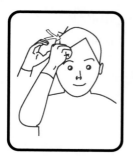

REMEMBER, MEMORY

R. full 'C' hand closes to a fist at side of head. May move down and tap on L. closed hand.

RENT, MORTGAGE

Irish T hand makes repeated forward movements from L. palm. Means **REGULAR PAYMENTS**.

REPLY, RESPOND, ANSWER

R. index near mouth flicks forward, as L. index held forward flicks back. *Directional*.

RESIDENTIAL, STAY OVER

Flat hands (or 'C' hands) at sides of head move forward/down twisting to palm down. Also means **BOARD/ING.**

RESPECT, HONOUR, OBEY

Flat hands touch forehead, then swing forward and down to finish palm up.

RESPONSIBLE, DUTY

Bent hands (or 'N' hands) one on top of the other, move down onto shoulder. Also means **DEPEND, RELY**.

REST, COMFORTABLE

Hands (or one hand) move back, thumbs onto chest, head tilted, lips pushed forward. Also means **BREAK, AT EASE, HOLIDAY**.

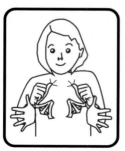

RETIRE/MENT, RELAX

Thumb tips of closed hands contact chest, then hands spring forward/open.

RICE

Palm back clawed hand shakes from side to side in front of chin. *Varies.*

RICH, WEALTHY

Edges of bent hands move down the body.

RIGHT, CORRECT

R. closed hand with thumb out moves down to contact L. palm

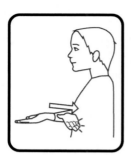

RIGHT, RIGHTS

Palm up hand moves back to contact lower chest.

RISK/Y, APPREHENSIVE

Tips of 'O hand tap into neck twice, lips stretched with teeth clenched.

RIVER, STREAM

'N' hands held apart move forwards with side to side wavy movements.

ROAD, STREET, WAY

'N' hands held apart twist from the wrists to point and move forward. Flat hands can be used. *Varies*.

ROOM, STUDIO

Index fingers move in square outline shape, or flat hands indicate room shape (see **BOX**). *Varies*.

ROTTEN, AWFUL, POOR

Edge of R. extended little finger rubs in circles on L. palm. Also means **DREADFUL, SHODDY.**

RUDE, BAD MANNERS

Tips of R. clawed hand rub up and down left upper arm. Also means **IMPOLITE**.

RUN, RUNNER, JOG/GER

Closed hands make alternate forward/up and down/back movements at sides of body.

SACK, DISMISS, FIRE

R. index fingers twists sharply forward from wrist, brushing against tip of L. index finger.
Directional.

SAD, DEPRESSED

Palm down R. flat hand moves down the body as shoulders and mouth droop. With 'phew' lip-pattern also means **RELIEF**.

SAD, SOLEMN, SERIOUS

Palm left R. flat hand moves down in front of nose. Mouth and shoulders droop.

SAFE, SAFETY, SECURE

R. bent hand on L. palm as hands move back to body.

293

SAILOR, NAVY, MARINE
Flat hands move together to touch right then left hip.

SALAD, TOSSED SALAD
'V' hands with thumbs out and slightly curved make circular tossing movements.

SALT, CRUMBLE
Thumb rubs across pads of fingers in crumbling action, or full 'C' hand twists over in action of shaking salt.

SAME, SIMILAR, LIKE

Index fingers pointing forward contact each other. May tap twice or make single contact.

SAND, EARTH, SOIL

Thumbs rub across pads of fingers in crumbling action as hands move upwards. Also means **FLOUR, POWDER**.

SANDWICH

Flat hands pat together twice, palm to palm. May twist over and repeat.

SAUSAGES

'N' hands open and close onto thumbs several times as hands move apart. One hand and one movement for **SAUSAGE**.

SAVE, SAVE UP, COLLECT

R. bent hand brushes back to body across L. palm.

SAY, REMARK, COMMENT

Index moves forward from the mouth, or full 'O' hands in front of body spring open twice, facing forward or back.

SCAN, ULTRASOUND

Edge of full 'O' hand moves round in circular movements on appropriate part of body.

SCANNER (computer)

R. 'Y' hand moves along L. palm, forward then back.

SCARF

Closed hands move in action of wrapping a scarf around the neck.

SCHOOL

Palm back flat hand makes side to side shaking movements in front of mouth. *Varies*.

SCHOOL

Palm forward 'N' hand shakes from side to side in front of mouth, and may also move down. *Varies.*

SCISSORS, CUT

Fingers of 'V' hand open and close twice.

SCORES, RESULTS

Fingers wiggle as palm back hands move alternately up and down. Also means **STATISTICS**.

SCOTLAND, SCOTTISH

Closed hand held in to body as elbow moves in and out several times.

SEA, OCEAN, WATER

Palm down open hand moves sideways in wavy up and down motion. Can be both hands.

SEARCH, LOOK FOR, SEEK

Hands make alternate circles forward/out near eyes, brows furrowed, head turns from side to side. Also means **HUNT**.

SEE, SIGHT

Index finger moves forward from eye. Can also be signed with 'V' hand (eye gaze classifier).

SEE YOU LATER

R. 'V' hand (or index finger) moves forward from eye, then index moves to the right in small arc.

SEED, SOW

Tips of R. 'O hand touch L. palm, then move forward/right in small arc, may repeat.

SEEM, SEEMS

Palm back flat hand swings forward/down from the face to finish palm up.

SELECT, PICK

Index finger closes onto thumb in backward movement, R. hand then L. and repeat.

SELF, MYSELF, ALONE

Index finger brushes downwards twice on chest.

SELL, SALE, SOLD

Tips of R. bent hand brush forward twice off L. palm. *Varies.*

SEND, THROW

Full 'O hand moves forward as fingers spring open. Also means **THROW OUT**. *Directional*.

SENSIBLE, THINK, BRAIN

Index finger taps side of forehead twice.

SENSITIVE, TOUCHY

Tip of R. middle finger makes small repeated brushing movement along back of L. hand.

SEPARATE, PART

Finger of bent hands back to back, then move apart. Also one version of **DIVORCE, SPLIT UP**. *Varies.*

SERIOUS, SAD, SOLEMN

Edge of R. flat hand moves down in front of nose, the mouth is turned down.

SERVICE/S, PROVIDE

Palm up flat hands move together from the right to the front of body. Also means **PROVISION.**

SEX, COITION, HAVE SEX

Closed hands are held palm facing, one above the other, and make repeated short movements towards each other. **Varies.**

SHARE, GIVE AND TAKE

R. flat hand on L. palm waggles from side to side as hands move backwards and forwards together. Means **SHARE USE OF.**

SHARE, PORTION, DIVIDE

Edge of R. flat hand taps along L. palm several times twisting forward from wrist. Means **SHARE OUT, SPLIT.**

SHAVE, RAZOR

Index edge of Irish 'T' hand brushes down cheek or appropriate part of body. Handshape can *vary*.

SHEEP, DERBY

Extended little fingers make forward circles from sides of head. Can be one hand or two.

SHEET, BEDSHEET

Two 'O' hands move up the body, or make forward shaking movement like spreading out a cloth.

SHOCK, ALARM, STARTLE

Tips of clawed hand make firm movement up body, or short firm movement forwards, with mouth open. *Varies.*

SHOE/S, SLIPPER/S

R. full 'C' hand palm down (or palm up) slots onto L. hand. Repeat L. onto R. for plural.

SHOP, SHOPPING

R. 'Y' hand on L. palm rubs from side to side. *Regional*.

SHOP, SHOPPING

Bent hands make two short downward movements in front of body. Also means **LONDON**. *Regional*

SHORT, LESS

Palm facing 'N' hands make short abrupt movement towards each other.

SHORTS, SHORT PANTS

Edges of flat hands tap twice on upper legs. Hands draw apart for **SHORT SKIRT, MINI**.

SHOULD, MUST, OUGHT

Palm down closed hand moves firmly left, twisting to palm left/back. With stretched lips means **BLAST, DAMN**.

SHOWER, HAVE SHOWER

Full 'O hand above head, bends down as fingers spring open several times.

SHY, BASHFUL, COY

Tip of R. index finger on chin as hand twists from palm left to palm back, head is down, or tilted.

SICK, THROW UP, VOMIT

Open hand brushes upwards on chest, and up past the mouth tipping forward to palm up.

SIGN, SIGN LANGUAGE

Open hands move in alternate forward circles. See also separate sign for **LANGUAGE**.

SILVER

Hands form fingerspelt 'S', then hands spring open and apart.

SING, SONG, CAROL

Palm back 'V' hand (or two hands) makes spiralling upward movements from near mouth.

SINGLE, NOT MARRIED

Fingers of R. flat hand brush down along back of L. hand fingers twice. *Regional*.

SISTER

R. bent index finger taps twice on nose, or flexes straight twice.

SIT DOWN

Palm down flat hands, one on top of the other, make short firm movement down.

SIT DOWN, CHAIR, SEAT

Fingers of R. bent 'V' hand (legs classifier) slot down over extended fingers of L. 'N' hand.

SKILL, EXPERTISE

R. hand with thumb up brushes sharply backwards across L. palm which twists forward at the same time.

SKY, HEAVENS

Bent hands move apart in small arc over the head.

SKY TV, SATELLITE

Tip of R. index finger contacts L. palm and bounces off again, pointing and moving downwards.

SLEEP, ASLEEP

Index fingers close onto thumbs at sides of eyes. Can be signed with all fingers closing onto thumbs.

SLOW, SLOWLY, AGES

R. hand brushes from left wrist up the forearm. Also means LONG TIME.

313

SLY, CHEAT, CRAFTY, LIE

Tip of thumb is drawn down the cheek, eyes narrowed and head tilted forward.

SMALL, SHORT, LITTLE

Palm down flat hand makes two short downward movements. Will *vary* in context.

SMART, DRESSY, SUIT

Thumb tips of closed hands (or 'Y' hands) move down chest.

SNOW, SNOWING

Fingers wiggle as hands move down in small wavy movements. Cheeks puffed for **HEAVY SNOW.**

SOCIAL WORKER

Fingertips of 'C' hands move down sides of chest. May repeat.

SOCK/S

'O' hands make short upward pulling movement near side of body for **SOCK**, and repeat at other side for plural.

SOFT, EASY, GENTLE

Index finger prods into the cheek twice. The cheeks may be puffed.

SOLDIER, ARMED FORCES

Edge of R. flat hand touches left, then right upper chest.

SOLICITOR, BARRISTER

Palm back 'V' hands move down and apart on upper chest. Fingers may flex.

SOLVE, DISSOLVE, MELT

Thumbs rub along pads of fingers as hands move apart slowly. Also means **SOLUTION**.

SOME, FEW, SEVERAL

Thumb rubs across pads of fingers.

SOMEONE, SOMEBODY

Upright index finger moves in horizontal circles.

SORRY, REGRET

Closed hand rubs in circular movements on the chest with sorrowful expression. Little finger may be extended.
Varies.

SORRY, REGRET

Flat hand rubs in circular movements on the chest with sorrowful expression.
Varies.

SOUP, CEREAL, DESSERT

Palm up 'N' hand (or Irish 'T' hand) makes repeated upward circular movements to the mouth from L. palm.

SPAIN, SPANISH

Palm back Irish 'T' hand on left upper chest twists over to palm forward. *Varies.*

SPECIAL, SUPERB

Palm forward 'O' hands make two short movements forward. One hand can be used.

SPECIAL/LY, SPECIALIST

R. index brushes forward sharply against L.

SPELL, SPELLING

Fingers and thumbs wiggle against each other as hands move to the right.

SPIDER

Fingers of palm down clawed hand wiggle as the hand moves forward.

SPORT

Closed hands with thumbs up pull apart diagonally with twisting movement from the wrists. *Varies.*

SPREAD, JAM, PASTE

Fingers of R. 'N' hand brush backwards and forwards in spreading action on L. palm.

SPRING, GROW, DEVELOP

R. open hand swivels from pointing down to being upright behind palm back L. flat hand. *Varies.*

STAND, WAIT

R. 'V' hand (legs classifier) stands on L. palm. Hands make short downward movements for **WAIT**.

START, BEGIN, COMMENCE

R. closed hand with thumb up moves sharply down behind L. flat hand.
Varies.

STAY, REMAIN, BE STILL

Palm down 'C' hands (or one hand) make short firm movement down or in *direction* of referent.

STOP, CEASE, END

Fingers of bent hand close onto thumb. Both hands can be used. Also means CONCLUDE, FINISH.
Varies.

STOP, WAIT, HOLD ON

Palm forward flat hand (or both hands) makes a short firm forward movement. Repeats for **WAIT, HOLD ON** etc. *Varies.*

STORM, GALE, STORMY

Flat hands at sides of head waft from side to side.

STORY, TALE, RELATE

Flat hands rotate round each other backwards or forwards (*directional*). Also means **GIVE ACCOUNT OF.**

323

STRAIGHT, DIRECT, GO

Flat hand bends forward from the wrist as it moves forward from in front of nose.

STRANGE, ODD, WEIRD

Index finger flicks out brushing across the chin. The nose is wrinkled and brows furrowed.

STRONG, ENERGY

Clenched fists move upwards as arms bend at the elbows. Arms may move out sideways. Also means **POWER**.

STRUCTURE, CONSTRUCT

Palm facing closed hands move alternately upwards, one on top of the other.

STUCK, BLOCK, JAM

Closed hands at right angles move firmly down, or same movement with bent index fingers linked together.

STUDY, READ

Palm back flat hands move together side to side several times.

SUBTITLES, CAPTIONS

Palm forward 'C' hands move apart. May repeat. *Varies.*

SUCCESS, SUCCEED, WIN

Irish 'T' hand twists in small circular movements at head height. *Varies*.

SUGAR, SPRINKLE

Palm up 'N' hand makes short repeated shaking side to side movements. *Varies.*

SUMMER

R. flat hand contacts chin, then moves upward in small arc to contact the forehead. *Regional.*

SUMMER, HOT WEATHER

Flat hand is drawn across the forehead. *Regional.*

SUN, SUNNY, SUNSHINE

Full 'O' hand moves down/in as the fingers spring open at head height.

SUPERMARKET, TROLLEY

Palm down fists move forward together.

SURE, DEFINITE, CERTAIN

Edge of R. flat hand bangs down onto L. palm.

SUSPECT, DON'T TRUST

'Y' hand makes short forward movements or in *direction* of referent, eyes narrowed. Also means **SUSPICIOUS**. *Varies*.

SWAP, REPLACE

'O' hands swap places
with each other
(***directional***). Handshape
may ***vary*** eg upright index
fingers (people).

SWEAR, BLAST, CURSE

Extended little finger
moves sharply forward
from mouth accompanied
by lip-pattern of swear
word, brows furrowed.

SWEET/S, TOFFEES

Index and thumb tips held
together tap side of mouth
twice.

SWIM, BREASTSTROKE

Flat hands move in forward circular movements, or arms move in overarm strokes for **SWIM, CRAWL**.

SWITCH OFF (mentally)

Irish 'T' hand twists sharply from palm forward to palm back at side of forehead. Same movement on neck for **SWITCH VOICE OFF**.

SWITCH, SWITCH ON/OFF

'O' hand twists up/back from the wrist in action of flicking a switch.

SWITZERLAND, SWISS

'C' hand makes short movement down, then across the chest in outline of a cross.

T SHIRT

Palm up flat hands tap upper arms twice, or rub in sideways movements. One hand can be used.

TABLE, LEVEL, PLATFORM

Palm down flat hands move apart.

TABLET, PILL

Index finger flicks off thumb twice towards the mouth.

TAKE, TAKEN, ADOPT

Palm down open or clawed hand moves in towards the body as hand closes in grasping action.

TALK, CHAT, CHATTER

Fingers of bent hand close onto thumb several times. Can change *direction* to suit context, and can be two hands.

TALK, CONVERSE, CHAT

Closed hands with index fingers extended bang R. on top of L. twice at right angles. Also means **DISCUSS**.

TAXI

Middle finger clicks against thumb several times, held at head height.

TEA, CAFE, CUP OF TEA

'O' hand moves up and tips slightly back to the mouth.

TEACH, EDUCATE

Bunched hands twist from temples and make two short forward movements. Also means **EDUCATION**. *Directional*.

TEACH/ER, INSTRUCT/OR

Index fingers near the mouth move forward, down and apart in two short movements. Also means **TUTOR**. *Directional*.

TECHNOLOGY

Palm back clawed hands swing down/in towards each other so that fingers intermesh. Also means **ENGINEER/ING**.

TEDDY, TEDDY BEAR

Closed hands are crossed and tap twice, hugging into chest. Clawed hands may be used.

TELEVISION, MONITOR

Index fingers move apart, down and back together in outline shape. Also means SCREEN, WINDOW.

TELL, MENTION, STATE

Index moves forward from the mouth, or full 'O' hands in front of body spring open twice, facing forward or back.

TEXT MESSAGE, SMS

Thumb flexes repeatedly as hand moves in small circles.

THANK YOU, APPRECIATE

Tips of flat hand touch mouth, then hand swings forward/down to finish palm up. Both hands can be used.

THAT'S ALL

Palm back open hands shake slightly down/apart twice. Also means **GOSH, WOW** if eyebrows are raised and lips rounded.

THEATRE, DRAMA, PLAY

Tip of R. middle finger on back of L. hand as R. hand wiggles side to side.   Also means **SHOW**.

THEIR/S, THEIR OWN

Palm forward closed hand sweeps round with eye gaze in *direction* of referents.

THEM, THEY, THOSE

Index finger pointing forward sweeps round in arc with eye gaze in *direction* of referents.

THING, SOMETHING, ITEM

Palm back closed hands with index fingers up bang together twice.

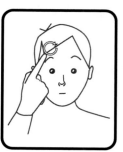

THINK, SUPPOSE

Index finger taps against, or makes small circles on side of forehead. Also means **WONDER.**

THIRSTY, FANCY, WISH

Fingers close onto thumb brushing forward twice off throat, or index finger moves down throat. Also means **DRY.**

THUNDER

Palm down open hands shake from side to side several times.

TICKET, CARD, PASS

Index fingers and thumbs extended and touching, move apart in outline shape. Also **RECEIPT, SLIP**. *Varies*.

TIDY, NEAT

Palm facing flat hands make short movement down, move sideways and repeat.

TIE, NECKTIE

'C' hands pull apart on front of chest.

TIME, WHAT TIME?

R. index taps back of left wrist twice. With brows raised or furrowed means **WHAT TIME?**

TINNITUS, HEAD NOISES

Irish 'T' hand makes small shaking movements near the ear.

TIRED, WORN OUT

Tips of bent hands on chest as hands flop downwards twisting from the wrists, cheeks puffed and head tilted. *Varies.*

TOAST, TOASTED

Bent hands make short movement down then up, or other *variation* in context.

TODAY, AT THE MOMENT

Palm up flat hands make two short movements down. Single firm movement for **AT ONCE.**

TOILET, TOILETS

Repeated fingerspelt 'T'.
Varies.

TOMATO

R. bunched hand twists against the end of L. index finger, or L. bunched hand.
Varies.

TOMORROW, NEXT DAY

Index finger on side of cheek twists forward/down from the wrist to finish palm up.

TOOTHBRUSH

Irish 'T' hand makes up and down brushing movements near the mouth. Also means **CLEAN (DO) ONE'S TEETH.**

TOSS AND TURN

R. 'V' hand (legs classifier) twists repeatedly from palm up to palm down on L. palm.

TOY/S

Hands in fingerspelt 'T' formation move in small circular movements. Also often fingerspelt.

TRAFFIC LIGHTS

Palm back full 'O' hand springs open, moves down and repeats twice.

TRAIN, LEARN, STUDY

Tips of bunched hands together as hands move forward/down twice. Also means **STUDENT, TRAINEE.** *Varies.*

TRAIN, LEARN, STUDY

R. flat hand brushes forward against L. twice. Also means **STUDENT, TRAINEE.** *Varies.*

TRAIN, RAILWAY

Closed hand (or fist) makes forward circular motions at side of body, or single firm movement forward.

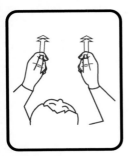

TREAT, TREATMENT, FEED

Palm in Irish 'T' hands make two short movements forward, or in *direction* of referent. Can twist and move back to signer.

TREE

R. open hand upright and resting on L. hand, twists repeatedly from the wrist.

TROUBLE, BOTHER, PEST

Tips of R. bent hand tap back of L. twice. Also means **NUISANCE** and one version of **NAUGHTY.**

TRUE, TRUST

Edge of R. flat hand bangs down on L. palm.

TRY, ATTEMPT

R. extended index finger brushes forward against L. May repeat.

TUTOR

Index fingers extended and pointing forwards are held R. on L. at an angle as hands make two short movements forward/down.

TV

Fingerspell 'TV'. *Varies.*

TYPETALK, RELAY CALL

'Y' hands swap round to change places.

347

UMBRELLA, BROLLY

R. Irish 'T' hand moves upwards from top of L.

UNCLE

R. index finger brushes in small repeated circular movement off tip of L. little finger. *Varies.*

UNDER

Palm up R. hand moves forward under palm down L hand in small arc.

UNDERSTAND, REALISE

Index finger flicks up at side of head. *Varies.*

UNEMPLOYED, NO WORK

R. flat hand chops down onto L. at right angles, then hands move apart, palm up with headshake.

UNFORTUNATELY

Closed hand moves slightly down and in with sharp twist from wrist, lips stretched, eyes narrowed. Also **BLAST, DAMN.**

UNION, STEWARD

Tips of bent 'V' hand and thumb tap left upper chest twice, or make small twisting movement. Also means **BADGE, BROOCH**.

UNIVERSITY

Index fingers twist round from sides of head to contact in front of forehead. Also one version of **COLLEGE**.

UNSURE, HESITANT

R. flat hand on L. palm makes wavering waggling movements from the wrist, lips are pressed together. Also means **DOUBTFUL**.

UP, UPWARDS, NORTH

Index finger points up and makes small upward movement. Repeated movement for **UPSTAIRS.**

UPSET, DISTRESSED

Open hand makes repeated upward brushing movements on upper chest.

US, WE

Index finger sweeps round in arc in front of body to finish on chest. Can be both hands moving apart.

USE, USEFUL

Fingers of bent hand and thumb stroke downwards off chin, closing to bunched hand, twice. *Varies*.

USE, USEFUL

Side of thumb brushes down twice off chin. Also *regional* MAN.

USHER'S SYNDROME

Flat hands at sides of head twist forward/in to indicate TUNNEL VISION.

VALUE, WORTH

Closed hands (or bunched hands) held together make two small movements forward/down. Also means **PRECIOUS**.

VEGETABLE, VEGETARIAN

Hands form fingerspelt 'V' with repeated movement, or fingerspelt abbreviation 'VEG'.

VIDEO

Palm down 'V' hands move in small horizontal circles. *Varies.*

VISIT, GO AND SEE

Palm back 'V' hands, slightly overlapping, move in short forward arc together. ***Directional. Varies.***

VOLUNTEER, INVITE/D

Tips of 'O' hand contact upper chest, then hand twists over and forwards, or tugs forward. Also means **BE CHOSEN, INVITATION.**

VOTE, ELECT

R. thumb and index fingertips draw a cross on L. palm. Extended index finger may be used. Also means **BAN, CANCEL.**

WAGE, PAY, SALARY

Fingers and thumb of R. bent hand close together as hand moves back down onto L. palm. R. clawed hand can be used.

WAIT

Palm down bent hands (or closed hands) make two short downward movements.

WALES, WELSH

Palm forward hand with index, middle and ring fingers extended, moves down as fingers flex.

WALK, ON FOOT, LEG IT

Fingers of R. bent 'V' (legs classifier) brush forward twice along L. palm or in *direction* to suit context. *Varies.*

WALK, ON FOOT, LEG IT

Fingers of 'V' hand (legs classifier) wiggle as hand moves forward or in *direction* to suit context. *Varies.*

WANT, NEED

Flat hand brushes down side of chest twisting to palm down.

WAR, BATTLE, CONFLICT

Fingers of open hands make short jabbing movements towards each other, or hands may move from side to side.

WARM

Clawed hand makes small circling movements in front of mouth. Flat hand can also be used. *Varies.*

WARNING, TELL OFF

Index finger makes two short waggling movements near side of head, brows furrowed. Also means **REBUKE, SCOLD.**

WASH HAIR, SHAMPOO

Clawed hands rub in circular movements on sides of head.

WASH, WASH HANDS

Hands rub together, or rub on appropriate part of body. Also means **SOAP**.

WATER, DRY, THIRSTY

Tips of flat or bent hand stroke twice down throat. For expanse of *water* see **SEA**. *Varies.*

WEAK, FEEBLE, FRAIL

Extended R. little finger brushes down left upper arm.

WEATHER, FRESH AIR

Bent hands waft backward near face several times. Also means **BREEZE, COOL.**

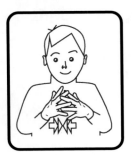

WEE WEE

Fingers form fingerspelt 'W' with two movements. Child appropriate sign.

WEEK, ONE WEEK

Extended index finger moves forward along left forearm. Two fingers extended for **TWO WEEKS** and so on.

WEEKEND

Hands form fingerspelt 'W' then closed hands come together.

WELCOME, RECEPTION

Flat hands bend backwards in short repeated movements. Also means **INVITATION**.

WELD, WELDING

'L' hand moves down with small wavy side to side movements.

WELL, FINE, HEALTH

Bent hands touch chest then move forward closing with thumbs up. With raised brows means **ARE YOU WELL?**

WET, DAMP, MOIST

Fingers of bent hand open and close onto thumb several times. Two hands can be used.

WHAT? WHAT FOR?

Palm forward index makes small side to side shaking movements, eyebrows raised or furrowed. Also *regional* WHY?

WHAT'S WRONG?

Extended little finger taps L. palm twice, eyebrows raised or furrowed. Also means **WHAT'S THE MATTER?**

WHEN?

Fingers wiggle at side of face, eyebrows raised or furrowed.

WHERE? WHEREABOUTS

Palm up hands move in small outward circles, or hands may move in-out towards each other, eyebrows raised or furrowed.

WHICH?

'Y' hand moves from side to side or between the objects or persons referred to, eyebrows raised or furrowed.

WHITBY, GRIMSBY, FISH

Thumb tip on chin as the fingers wiggle (*regional*).

WHITE

Tips of 'O' hand (or index tip) make small repeated brushing movements near the collar.
Colours can vary widely.

WHO?

Palm left R. index fingertip taps chin twice, eyebrows raised or furrowed.
Varies.

WHO?

Index finger makes small horizontal circles, eyebrows raised or furrowed. *Varies.*

WHY?

Edge of R. index taps side of left upper chest twice, eyebrows raised or furrowed.

WIDE, WIDTH

Open hands move apart.

WILD, UNTAMED

Extended little finger makes circular movements on side of forehead, eyes narrowed. Also one version of **SUSPECT, SUSPICIOUS.**

WILL, SHALL, WOULD

Palm forward closed hand twists to palm down at side of chin.

WIN, SUCCEED, ACHIEVE

R. clawed hand brushes left across L. palm grasping sharply closed. Can be R. hand only at head height. *Varies*.

WIND, WINDY, GUSTY

Palm back open hands waft back to face several times, or in *direction* to suit context.

WINDOW

R. palm back flat hand moves up and down on top of L. *Varies.*

WINE

Thumb of 'Y' hand moves up to mouth as hand tips backwards.

WIRE, STRING

Tips of 'O' hands in contact, then hands move apart in twisting movement.

WITH, TOGETHER

Fingers of L. 'N' hand hold fingers of R. 'N' hand. *Varies.*

WOLVERHAMPTON

Bent hand with thumb out moves forward/down in front of nose closing to a bunched hand. Also means **WOLF.**

WOMAN, FEMALE, LADY

Palm forward index finger brushes forward twice across cheek. *Varies.*

WON'T, WILL NOT

Palm forward 'O' hand springs open in forward movement, as the head shakes.

WOOD, WOODEN

Thumb tip scrapes downwards on L. palm twice twisting from the wrist.

WORD

Palm forward 'C' hand makes short movement forward.

WORK, CAREER, JOB

Edge of R. flat hands makes short forward tapping movements on L. at right angles. Also means **EMPLOYMENT**.

WORLD, EARTH

Open hands with fingers slightly curved twist out apart and down to finish touching each other.

WORM, SLUG

Palm left R. index finger flexes repeatedly as hand moves forward/left. Also *regional* version of **MOUSE, RAT**.

WORRY, CONCERN

Clawed hands twist in/down over eyes or move in alternating circles. Also means **ANXIETY**. *Varies.*

WORSE/N, DETERIORATE

R. little finger brushes downwards twice off L. little finger, or little fingers move down/apart. Brows are furrowed.

WORST, FAIL, LAST

R. little finger brushes sharply down against L. Brows are furrowed.

WOW, GOSH

Palm back open hands shake slightly down/apart twice. Eyes are wide open, and lips rounded.

WRITE, PEN AND PAPER

R. 'O' hand moves along L. palm with squiggling movements. Also means **SIGN FOR, TAKE NOTES**.

WRONG, FAULT, SIN

Edge of R. little finger bangs down on L. palm. May repeat. Or can be R. hand only *directed* to referent in context.

YEAR, YEARS

Hands form fingerspelt 'Y' with small downward brushing movement. Repeat for **YEARS.**

YELLOW

Fingerspell 'Y' and make small repeated brushing movements with R. index. **Colours can vary widely.**

YES (affirmation)

The head nods. Can accompany statement to confirm agreement.

YES, YES, OF COURSE

R. closed hand (head classifer) nods twice resting on L. index, as head also nods. Used mainly in reported speech.

YESTERDAY, DAY BEFORE

Index finger on side of cheek twists back/down onto shoulder. With 'V' hand means **TWO DAYS AGO**.

YOU

Index points with short movement towards referent (with eye gaze). Sideways sweep for plural. *Directional*.

YOU'RE RIGHT

Closed hand with thumb out makes two short forward movements, or in *direction* of referent.

YOUNG

Hands form fingerspelt 'Y' with repeated brushing movement. *Varies.*

YOUR, YOURS

Palm forward closed hand is directed towards referent (with eye gaze). Sideways sweep for plurals. *Directional.*

YOURSELF, HIM/HERSELF

Palm back index held forward makes short movements down/forward in *direction* of referent.

YOURSELVES

Index held forward moves down, then to right and repeats, or both hands moving alternately. Also means **THEMSELVES**.

ZERO, NIL, NOUGHT

Full 'O' hand (or 'O' hand) held in front of body makes short movement forward. Also means **NOTHING**.

AMERICAN ONE-HANDED FINGERSPELLING ALPHABET

A	B
C	D
E	F
G	H
I	J
K	L
M	N
O	P
Q	R
S	T
U	V
W	X
Y	Z

© 2005 **DEAFSIGN** www.deafsign.com From the LET'S SIGN SERIES, may be copied as reminder sheet.

SOURCES AND
RECOMMENDED READING

British Deaf Association
(1992)
Dictionary of British Sign Language/English.
London: Faber and Faber.

Klima, E. and Bellugi, U.
(1979)
The Signs of Language. Harvard University Press.

Rachel Sutton-Spence and Bencie Woll
(1999)
The Linguistics of British Sign Language:
An Introduction. Cambridge University Press.

The LET'S SIGN Series
British Sign Language Resources
(2001 - present)
Co-Sign Communications (DEAFSIGN).
(See details and images at the back of the book)

Available in libraries and bookshops and by
mail-order from Forest Books (details page370).

British Association of Teachers of the Deaf (BATOD)

175 Dashwood Avenue,
High Wycombe,
Buckinghamshire HP12 3DB.
Answerphone/Fax: 01494 464190
e-mail: secretary@batod.org.uk
web: www.batod.org.uk

British Deaf Association (BDA)

Coventry Point, Market Way, Coventry CV1 1EA.
Tel/Voice: 020 75883520
Tel/Text: 020 75883529
Fax: 020 75883527
Videophone: 020 74969539
Helpline Textphone: 0800 6522965
e-mail: helpline@bda.org.uk
web: www.signcommunity.org.uk

Council for the Advancement of Communication with Deaf People (CACDP)

Durham University Science Park,
Block 4, Stockton Road, Durham DH1 3UZ.
Tel: 0191 383 1155 (V/T)
Text: 0191 383 7915   **Fax:** 0191 383 7914
e-mail: durham@cacdp.org.uk
web: www.cacdp.org.uk

DEAFSIGN

(British Sign Language Information and Resources)
16 Highfield Crescent, Hartburn,
Stockton on Tees TS18 5HH.
Tel: 01642 580505 (V/T) **Fax:** 01642 808959
e-mail: cath@deafsign.com
web: www.deafsign.com

Forest Books

(Specialists in Books, Videos, CD-Roms on sign
language/deaf issues)
The New Building, Ellwood Road, Milkwall, Coleford,
Gloucestershire GL16 7LE.
Tel: 01594 833858 (V/T)
Videophone: 01594 810637 **Fax:** 01594 833446
e-mail: forest@forestbooks.com
web: www.ForestBooks.com

The Royal National Institute for Deaf People (RNID)

19-23 Featherstone Street,
London EC1Y 8SL.
Tel: 020 7296 8000 (V) 020 7296 8001 (T)
Fax: 020 7296 8199
Information line:
Tel: 0808 808 0123 (freephone)
Textphone: 0808 808 9000 (freephone)
e-mail: informationline@rnid.org.uk
web: www.rnid.org.uk

TYPETALK: National Telephone Relay Service

Helpline 0800 500 888 (text) 0800 7311 888 (voice)
0151 709 8119 (fax)

BT TextDirect.
Users can dial directly to the person they want to speak to.
Text users dial **18001;** Voice users **18002;** then the area
code and number wanted.

In emergencies:
Textphone users can dial **18000 (no other number
needed)**.
This number alone connects a call to the emergency
services and a Typetalk Operator will join the line to
help relay the call.
e-mail: helpline@rnid-typetalk.org.uk
web: www.typetalk.org

Useful Websites

www.artsigns.ac.uk
www.bbc.co.uk/seehear
www.bsl-infoweb.org
www.deaf247.co.uk
www.deafclub.co.uk
www.diseed.org.uk

www.handsonaccess.com
www.learnbsl.org
www.britishsignlanguage.com
www.royaldeaf.org.uk
www.signingbabes.co.uk
www.underfives.co.uk

INDEX

385

386

391

393

394

397

SERIES

Informative, fun and educational
British Sign Language (BSL) Resources.
Compatible with all educational sign systems based on BSL.

Developed by Deaf and hearing contributors in response to the
need for more and better BSL materials for schools, the home and
in Adult Education. For all ages and abilities - in the field of
deafness, special needs and for signing with hearing
babies and children.
Informed by many years experience within the British Deaf
community and education.

A2 POSTER
BSL GREETINGS SIGNS and Fingerspelling

Bold • Eye-catching • Laminated

For Nurseries, Schools, Colleges, Hospitals
and all Public Buildings.

Suitable for anywhere and everywhere.

A4 POSTER/MATS - Set of 4

Colourful wipe-clean and in topics.

**Greetings • Family
Feelings • Questions**

Also available in
Bengali • Gujarati • Urdu• German

EARLY YEARS & BABY SIGNS

A3 POSTERS Set of 2

Laminated - 17" x 12.5"

48 most useful **First Signs** for babies and young children. Signs include **'bath' 'bed' 'milk' 'more' 'cuddle'.**

Reminder charts for the wall or wipe-clean placemats.

With A4 Keepsake sheet to fill in and keep.
For the home, nursery and pre-school environments.

Also available on **FLASHCARDS**

48 cards (4" x 6") **First Signs**

Large image of sign and word on one side.
Fingerspelt word and description on reverse.

NEW (2005) BSL THANK YOU CARDS

Quality cards with Fingerspelling Alphabet on the back.

In pack of 6 **A6** (4"x 5.75")
OR pack of 10 **A7** (4"x 3")

Pink/Red and Blue/Purple with white envelopes.

LET'S SIGN EARLY YEARS
BSL Child and Carer Guide

Excellent introduction to BSL by Deaf and hearing co-writers.
A5 comb-bound or paperback 132 pages

* **300** child appropriate signs
  with variations
* Examples of signed phrases
* Numbers up to ten
* Captions to describe how
  each sign is made
* Left and Right handed
  Fingerspelling Alphabets
* Useful Contacts and full Index

Suitable for families and all those whose work brings contact with
young children from babyhood onwards - deaf children, children
with special needs and Baby Signing with hearing children.

LET'S SIGN FOR WORK
BSL Guide for Service Providers

To improve access in compliance with the Disability
Discrimination Act.
A5 Comb-Bound 76 pages

* Over **170** appropriate signs
  and variations
* Clear communication advice
  and background
* Captions to describe how each
  sign is made
* Useful Contacts and full Index